Building Christian
Communities

Building Christian Communities

Strategy for Renewing the Church

STEPHEN B. CLARK

AVE MARIA PRESS

Notre Dame, Indiana 46556

Nihil Obstat: John L. Reedy, C.S.C.
        Censor Deputatus

Imprimatur: Most Rev. Leo A. Pursley, D.D.
        Bishop of Fort Wayne-South Bend

© 1972 by *Cursillos in Christianity in the
United States of America.* All rights reserved

Library of Congress Catalog Card Number: 75-189990

International Standard Book Number: 9-87793-042-2 (cloth)
International Standard Book Number: 0-87793-043-0 (paper)

Photograph by Jean-Claude Lejeune

Published 1972 by Ave Maria Press

Printed in the United States of America

Contents

Introduction

The president of the Holy Name won't go to the folk
Mass because it's sponsored by "those cursillistas" . . .
a priest is jailed in a civil rights demonstration . . . a
survey in a Catholic high school discloses that only a
minority of the students have been to confession in the
last three years . . . a Pentecostal meeting becomes the
latest "thing" in a diocese, packing the parish hall each
week . . . the rector of a seminary leaves the priesthood
. . . a diocese gives many of its top officials a management training course . . . a Trappist monastery institutes
"dialogues" . . . a daily communicant, faithful to the
Church and its clergy for years, announces that she will
not go back to Mass because the priests in her parish
have "lost the faith" . . . a weekend retreat becomes so
popular with high school students that it cannot accommodate all the applicants.

Change in the Church, crisis in the Church. Ten
years ago people were still seriously talking about the
Church being a monolith. Only ten years ago — and

already it seems like the primeval beginning of a new era — the Catholic bishops of the United States went to the Second Vatican Council and boasted about the strength and solidity of American Church life: the growth in the schools, the increasing number of converts, the strength of the priesthood and sisterhood. Now each of these is a major crisis area, and there is even hushed talk of the possibility of the disintegration of the American Church.

The seeds of change were slow in sprouting. For many years the Church managed to remain stable and tranquil; it avoided being caught up in the increasingly rapid changes in American society caused by modern technetronic progress. But no longer. Now it is in the middle of a rapid social change. It is, in fact, changing faster than most other groupings in American society. It is like a log that had been bumping along on the side of a stream and then suddenly pushed off into the current and now finds itself in the middle of the stream, rushing along, crashing off rocks, shooting down rapids.

A sociologist could have predicted what would happen when the change came about in the Church (are there any who actually did?). Social upheavals produce confusion, loss of morale, paralysis. People become disoriented and confused, uncertain about where to move, insecure about the value of things that once seemed so unquestionably important. The Church is suffering today from loss of morale and, in many areas, a paralysis. What has happened is understandable, but nonetheless hard to deal with.

The situation in the Church is not all bleak, by any means. Many good and constructive things are happening. But despite all the good, there is still an overall loss of a sense of direction. There are few hints of any overall progress. Most of the good things (and most of the bad things) which are happening in the Church seem more in the nature of reactions: attempts to improve this situation, to stem that tide, to make some contribution. It is difficult to see that something is being built, that there is an overall vision and approach with a good chance of getting somewhere.

A direction is needed, a plan, a strategy. These are all different words for the same reality. This book is concerned with pastoral planning or pastoral strategy. It is an attempt to state what the main lines of the overall approach of workers (priests, nuns, lay people) in the Church should be. An "overall approach" involves taking stock of the whole situation of the Church and trying to understand what should be done to make advances in the whole situation. Too often workers in the Church are content to do whatever good things they find to do. They do not ask what can be done to make headway, where the priorities are, how the difficulties of the Church as a whole can be tackled.

The approach developed in this book has sources. The bibliography contains books in which more can be read about the ideas discussed. But the approach has come mainly from experience, from what I have seen happening in our own community, as well as from my experience in working in two parishes and three national movements. The book has been written because the ideas have been shown to work.

The approach suggested in this book has some unique perspectives. Not that the ideas are entirely new: As a matter of fact, they stand in a certain tradition of Catholic pastoral thought — a tradition marked by such names as Abbe Michonneau, Cardinal Suenens, Bishop Hervas, Juan Capo, Eduardo Bonin, Max Delespasse, Leo Mahon. But the approach is "unique" in that most American Catholics do not think this way.

If a person were to read the pages of the Catholic papers or magazines he would soon come to think that the main problems facing the Church today are issues such as clerical celibacy, authority and conscience, birth control, or perhaps institutions (parish councils, elected bishops, the reorganization of the curia) or programs (community development projects, ecumenical dialogues, parent-educator plans). Yet, this book does not consider any of these. They are not the most fundamental or basic questions facing the Church.

A logical question is: If the basic questions are not in the area of issues, institutions, or programs, where are they? The viewpoint this book takes is that what the Church needs today more than new institutions or programs are vital Christian communities. As seen from this perspective, the basic questions lie in the area of voluntary social organization and in what could be called "environmental dynamics." What this means will be clearer as we proceed, but it involves such ideas as the following: a) environments and communities are more important than institutions in the life of the Church, b) a "naturally emergent" leadership is the kind of leadership which the Church needs, c) religious renewal is *functionally* central to the renewal of the Church and therefore a *practical* necessity, and d) movements in the Church are not an obstacle but essential to the survival of the Church and therefore should be fostered.

The basic insight of this book will be developed by explaining five theses about the way of improving the overall situation in the Church today. The theses are:

1) The main goal of pastoral efforts in the Church today is to build communities which make it possible for a person to live a Christian life.

2) The Church should be restructured to form basic Christian communities.

3) Vital Christian communities are formed only through centering upon Christ (through spiritual renewal).

4) The Church today needs leaders who can work with an environmental approach.

5) Constructive social change in the Church today should be fostered through the intelligent use of movements.

1

The Holistic Approach

People working in the Church today often do not have an overall pastoral approach. Most have either an activities-oriented approach or a problem-oriented approach. I have found myself in the last few years in a number of working groups in the Church. In literally hundreds of meetings—trying to do anything in the modern world gives a person a great deal of experience with meetings — these groups have almost always dealt with activities or problems; rarely have they reached the level of an overall approach or strategy for building up the Church.

Perhaps the most common approach in the Church today is activities-oriented. For instance, a parish staff meeting will regularly concern itself with getting teachers for the CCD program, scheduling Masses, repairing buildings, getting commentators and lectors, registering children for school. It will consider these important because it is assumed that every parish must have certain activities. Therefore the function of those in charge of the parish is to see that these activities happen. They must be scheduled and given a place, and people must be found for them. It is sometimes assumed, in fact, that the more activities a parish has, the better that parish is.

Another example which illustrates the activities-oriented approach concerns the training a priest gets. Most of a priest's education is academic, but when he is given practical training, he is taught how to speak (give sermons), how to perform the liturgy, how to teach catechism, perhaps how to counsel. In other words, his practical training consists in being given skills to perform certain activities well. His practical training is activities-oriented.

The second most common approach is the problem-oriented approach (not to be confused with what some sociologists term the "problem-solving approach," which is, in fact, close to what will later be described as the holistic approach). The parish staff meeting can also illustrate the problem-oriented approach. The parish staff meeting will often take up a number of problems: how to accommodate the people for the Mass with the overflow crowds, how to handle the situation now that there is one less priest, how to get more children to attend CCD, what to do now that not enough volunteer teachers showed up, or how to respond to the boycott. Much of what happens in a parish staff meeting is re-action — responding to a particular problem which has to be solved.

The training which priests receive can also illustrate the problem-oriented approach. Because of the many new problems facing the Church today, many efforts are being made to improve the formation of priests. The

13

inner-city problem, the education problem, the problems of authority and structure, all need attention. The response on the part of many priests and seminarians and on the part of those forming priests often is to want to add to priestly training the study of social work, counseling, or sometimes politics (some priests, for instance, are "going to school" to Saul Alinsky and others to learn how to help their people or even to learn how to deal with their bishops). There is a natural desire for priests and those forming them to want to add particular skills to help them deal with particular problems.

A third approach is the holistic approach. This approach has to be concerned with activities and problems, but it does not put the focus there. The focus in the holistic approach is on the *goal* or *ideal* and on the *whole*. In other words, the holistic approach is primarily interested in building something, in forming the Church as a whole or some unit of the Church into what it should become. Someone who is working with the holistic approach would keep his interest mainly focused on the goal or ideal of what the Church should be and on the Church (or part of it) as a whole. He would work toward having a process under way which would move it toward becoming what it should be.

The three different approaches can be illustrated in house construction. In building a house there are a number of activities needed. There are the carpentry work, the electrical work, the painting. One man runs a bulldozer leveling the ground, another makes concrete for the foundations, still another raises the beams. These are all activities which are essential for building the house, and the people who perform them usually take an activities-oriented approach. They have "a job to do." Also, in the construction of a house, problems need to be dealt with. Steel beams are too long. A sudden rain floods the basement. These are specific problems that can develop, and they can be taken care of by a problem-oriented approach. The foreman calls in special help or equipment to take care of the specific problem.

In addition to all the activities and the efforts that deal with problems, there is also the work of the architect. He has what might be called the holistic approach in the construction of houses. He is concerned that all the activities and efforts go together in such a way that something is being built. He is concerned with the goal, with the whole.

Both the activities-oriented approach and the problem-oriented approach embody the danger of just considering an activity in itself. In the holistic approach, on the other hand, it is clear that the activity has to be considered and evaluated primarily in its place in the whole and in its relationship to the purpose of the whole.

An activities-oriented approach or a problem-oriented approach is adequate in situations where there is little overall change, because in those situations the specifications of the job are obvious. They can be learned as a set of activities. For example, a number of years back, a person could be taught how to function as a priest with an activities-oriented approach. What had to happen at a Mass, for instance, seemed relatively obvious. All the person had to do was to learn a set of skills. The specifications were visible and could be handled with a little experience.

When a process of development is needed, however, the use of only an activities-oriented approach or a problem-oriented approach can lead to a variety of difficulties. Sometimes the efforts made turn out to be aimless or block the development which should take place. A progressive priest, for example, will decide that changes have to be made for the renewal of a parish. He will then go about introducing all the good things he has seen. He will establish CFM groups, send people to Cursillos, begin folk liturgies, have dialogue groups, start a parish council, cosponsor a sensitivity-type weekend and "open up" the rectory. Within a couple of years, he and his people will begin to develop battle fatigue, because they are involved in a number of activities without those activities adding up to anything or without the parish being formed into some kind of whole. Moreover, the existence of different groups and programs that people are committed to will block the development of the right kind of efforts, because the people who should be responsible for a better parish life have their time taken up in activities which are good, but which do not add up to a better parish.

The holistic approach is needed also when the situation as a whole is inadequate and needs a total redesigning. Often in dealing with problems, it can be a mistake to focus only on the problems themselves, the way a problem-oriented approach does. Focusing on the problems can lead to solutions which meet the problem but are destructive to the whole effort. For instance, one criticism leveled against housing projects in cities is that, in destroying old neighborhoods, they cause worse social problems than the one they relieve (inadequate housing), because they uproot people and destroy the help people get from natural community patterns. If this is true, building housing projects is an example of solving a problem and making the situation in the city as a whole worse.

Sometimes focusing on problems can lead to working on particular solutions when what is needed is an overall strategy which, while not dealing with each problem in itself, eliminates the need to deal with them because it eliminates the cause. Take, for instance, some approaches for dealing with the problems patients have in a mental hospital. Institutional settings cause certain problems as well as relieving others (as was discovered after hospitals were built). One approach to handling these problems is to add new types of counseling and other new services (both costly procedures). An alternate approach, for at least a variety of patients, is to develop treatments which involve the patient's living outside an institution and needing less care. In other words, the new approaches which are being worked out are not just a matter of patching up the old system (solving its individual problems), but taking a look at the whole and trying to redesign it (a new strategy).

What we have called the holistic approach becomes more and more important in times of rapid social change. Today one of the most significant developments in business is the so-called "managerial revolution." A hundred years ago, business was conceived of as the operation of a certain number of activities. The job of the owner or top man was mainly that of making sure everything got done. But in today's rapidly changing economy, the key person in the business is the manager, the person who can grasp the goals of the operation and who can mold the entire business or part of it into a whole, a unit, which can pursue its goals and adapt to the changes of society without disintegrating or becoming less and less effective (less and less profitable). Today's manager has to have a holistic approach.

The Church today is being forced to go through the same process which business is going through. It needs a pastoral revolution similar to the managerial revolution in business. One hundred years ago, it was obvious in the Church what needed doing. There was a system that worked tolerably well. As long as the priest learned some skills so he could perform certain activities, the Church would go on. It was enough for the priest, say, to learn how to teach catechism better. He would never have to face the situation in which people would be asking why have catechism at all. The activities of a parish could be listed and a man could be trained for any or all of them.

I do not mean to say that the holistic approach was not needed a hundred years ago in the Church, any more than that businesses did not need managers then. The holistic approach was needed to set up the system in the first place and to deal with any problems that came up which were of such magnitude that some major adjustment was needed to deal with them. Moreover, if a priest back then had a holistic approach, he could do a great deal more for a parish. But the holistic approach was not needed then nearly as much as it is now. A man without a holistic approach could get by if he could do the activities well enough and was a likeable enough person. Now that is less and less true. Every unit of the Church needs people with a holistic approach. It is no accident that now people are anxious about the role of the priest and the purpose of the parish. The old system cannot be simply assumed. It is changing. People are needed who can be the managers of a process of Church renewal. People are needed who can grasp the purpose of the Church, who can care for the whole Church, who can build something.

The holistic approach gives us the vantage point from which to ask what are the most important tasks facing the Church today. It is not enough to deal with the problems (clerical celibacy, papal authority, birth control). Nor is it enough to develop new activities (parish councils, ecumenical dialogues, parent-educator programs). These may be important, but they can be handled only in the context of an overall strategy or blueprint for building the Church. What is needed is a clear grasp of the goal (what it is that we are trying to do in the Church today, what ideal the Church should be heading for) and a way of bringing the Church as a whole (the whole Church) to it. What is needed is a plan of development that will deal with the needs of the Church in the 20th-century world.

2

The Pastoral Goal--
Community

What, then, is the goal, the vision of the Church, that can guide a process of development and of restructuring? It can be stated as follows:

The main goal of the pastoral efforts in the Church today is to build communities which make it possible for a person to live a Christian life.

In the letter to the Ephesians, St. Paul talks about the purpose of Christianity. Or, to use other words, he talks about God's intention in sending Christ (Christianity is something God initiated and told men about, not something men thought up and proposed to God):

> For he has made known to us in all his wisdom and insight the mystery of his will, according to his purpose which he set forth in Christ as a plan for the fullness of time, to unite all things in him, things in heaven and things on earth. In him, according to the purpose of him who accomplished all things according to the counsel of his will, we who first hoped in Christ have been destined and appointed to live for the praise of his glory . . .
>
> So then you are no longer strangers and sojourners,

but you are fellow citizens with the saints and members of the household of God, built upon the foundation of the apostles and prophets, Christ Jesus himself being the cornerstone, in whom the whole structure is joined together and grows into a holy temple in the Lord; in whom you are also built into it for a dwelling place of God in the Spirit (Eph. 1:9-12, 2:19-22).

Three ideas contained in this section of Paul's letter are of particular importance for considerations of pastoral planning:

1) God did and still does have a purpose for creation and redemption and if we miss that purpose, we miss what we were made for.

2) God's purpose, in respect to the human race, was to create a people who were united with him, to create a unity of God and man, one body (including God), a temple (in whom God's Spirit dwells).

3) Man's purpose is to live for the praise of God's glory (or, as it is put in the *Constitution on the Church in the Modern World,* sec. 24, "all men are called to one and the same goal, namely, God himself").

It is possible to see things from God's perspective in our pastoral work—possible not because we are naturally capable of it, without running the risk of serious distortion — but because God has revealed to us how he thinks, and what his purpose is. If we do not keep God's intention before our minds, we run the risk, to use a Pauline phrase, of "running in vain" (Gal. 2:12).

It is from God's purpose, then, that the goal of pastoral work should be drawn. God's purpose is to build a people united with him (a people of God), a body of Christ, a temple of the Holy Spirit. A Christian worker should have the same purpose as God's — to build something — to work to form a people who live for God. This should be the result of all pastoral work.

Here an important distinction comes in. There is a difference between the goal of pastoral work and the goal of Christian life. The goal of Christian life is to "live for the praise of God's glory." The goal of pastoral work is to build a people of God. An individual's prayer life may be important to his life as a Christian, but it is not one of the activities of his pastoral work (unless, of course, his prayer is being specifically directed to building up the people of God). The goal of pastoral work is to form a people who will do all the things which Christians should do.

This distinction has some practical importance in understanding what we are considering. Teaching biology may be a good thing, the kind of thing a Christian should do. But if a priest decides to teach biology, he is no longer doing pastoral work. (This is not to imply that he is automatically wrong in going into teaching biology — only that he is no longer doing pastoral work.) In other words, there are many activities which can be part of the Christian life which are not the work of someone engaged in pastoral work.

The goal of pastoral work, then, is to build a people who live for God, a body of Christ. Or, rephrased, the goal of pastoral work is to form communities which live for God, Christian communities. There is a reason (for the purpose of this book) for using the word "community" rather than the word "people." For a modern American, the word "community" makes clear that what is involved is a matter of social organization, a meaning which the word "people" carried in the ancient world but which it no longer does, or at least not so clearly.

Even though a different word is used, the meaning is the same. If Christianity is going to change men, it is going to have to realign social relationships. To think of "Christianizing the world" exclusively in terms of getting certain principles accepted or certain values accepted, or even in terms of getting individuals to have a relationship with Christ, would be to miss one of the basic realities of human nature — that human beings do not function independently; they change in groups. The target has to be to form Christian communities, Christian social groupings.

To understand, therefore, why the main goal of pastoral efforts in the Church today must be to build communities which make it possible for a person to live a Christian life, it is necessary to affirm three principles:

1) that a person's beliefs, attitudes, values and behavior patterns (and hence his Christianity) are formed to a great degree by his environment, and therefore the normal person needs a Christian environment if he is going to live Christianity in a vital way,

2) that environmental factors are more basic than institutional factors in Christian growth and therefore the primary pastoral concern should be in forming Christian environments rather than in reforming Christian institutions, and

3) that when society as a whole cannot be expected to accept Christianity, it is necessary to form

communities within society to make Christian life possible.

THE IMPORTANCE OF "ENVIRONMENT"

(1) A person's beliefs, attitudes, values and behavior patterns (and hence his Christianity) are formed to a great degree by his environment, and therefore the normal person needs a Christian environment if he is going to live Christianity in a vital way.

"Environment" can be used in a broad sense to indicate all the factors in a human being's surroundings (climate, soil, atmospheric pressure, etc.), but in a narrower sense, it refers only to the social setting a human being finds himself in. If a person lives among people who accept Christianity, he lives in a Christian environment. If a person works with people involved in a great deal of conflict with one another, he has a turbulent work environment. If a person goes to school with people who use drugs frequently, he has a school environment that is characterized by heavy drug use.

Environments form in many situations. A family is an environment, as is a group of friends. A school provides a place for environments to form, as does a parish or a business. The sisters in the convent, the teachers at the school, a gang of eighth-graders, and the men of the St. Vincent de Paul Society are all examples of environments that might exist within a parish. There are usually a number of environments in a person's life — his family, his work situation, the group of friends he spends time with, perhaps the people in a religious or civic organization of which he is a part.

An environment is formed when a group of people

interrelate or interact. The people on a bus do not form an environment, because they do not interact. They are simply an aggregate. Often the families in a neighborhood or an apartment house (especially in a big city or town with a large transient population) do not form an environment. They rarely talk to one another, do things for one another (or to one another), or get to know one another. They do not become involved with one another in any important part of their lives.

An environment is a social situation that has some kind of stability. Three people who meet on the way to work and talk for a half hour do not form an environment. A group of people in a construction company who just happen to be together for an afternoon on a particular job do not form an environment. An environment is formed when people relate to each other in a consistent, regular way — when they live together or work together or play together or spend time together for any reason in an ongoing way. The environments in our lives are the places where we have some involvement with the same people daily or weekly or monthly.

An environment, then, could be defined as a stable social situation or a stable pattern of interaction between human beings. Later on, when the difference between an environment and an institution is considered, another element will be added to the definition. For the present purposes, the definition of an "environment" involves three elements 1) it is stable (involving an ongoing grouping) 2) it is a pattern of interaction 3) it involves human beings.

There are various degrees of interaction in an environment. Some environments are more intense than others, that is, they involve more interaction among the members. A family (usually) is a more intense environment than a ladies' guild. Some environments are more cohesive than others, that is, the members feel more drawn to one another. They spend more time with one another voluntarily, are more open to one another, and have more of an influence on one another. Some environments are more total than others, that is, they involve more aspects of a person's life. A cloistered convent is more total than a family (although the family could be more intense or more cohesive).

There are also various levels of environments. There are levels according to size. Environments can be formed of a large number of people (the university environment, for example) or a small number of people (the family). There are also levels according to geography. Environments can be formed on a local level (in a neighborhood or a town), or on a regional or national or international level (there is an international environment formed by the Cursillo movement, as there is an international environment formed by devoted mountain climbers).

Environments always have commonly accepted attitudes or values. What these are varies according to the environment. For instance, at a university today, certain academic values might be held (values which stress scholarship, for instance) and also perhaps certain political values (universities tend to be more opposed to the war in Vietnam) and social values (a man with long hair can feel much more acceptance at the university than he can back home in the suburbs). Not everyone in an environment might agree with all of the

26

attitudes or values which are characteristic of it, but these values are what are generally accepted and they set the tone. Hence, when a student comes to the university, he will be more likely to become liberal and to wear his hair long than he would at home.

Environments have a great deal of effect on a person. To a great extent, what a man is is determined by the environments he finds himself in. The fact that he grew up in a certain family marks him for the rest of his life. Knowing that he is a middle-class American rather than a Burmese peasant is enough to tell a great deal about him. It is not true, of course, to say that a person is completely determined by his environments because he has a certain degree of choice between the different environments he is in, and he has the choice about how he is going to relate to each environment.

For many people it is hard to grasp the strength of the influence of various environments. They tend to think that they, and other men, proceed mainly by gathering information, weighing it, and making decisions about what they are going to think and do. This is part of the way people function, but it is not the whole story.

There are many everyday facts which demonstrate the effect of environments on people, facts which even people who know no sociology instinctively realize. A mother, for instance, is careful about the children her children hang around with. She knows that they will have an influence on her children and that her children will tend to act like them. We might remember the effect a certain group had upon us in youth. Perhaps we went through a political change that came from hanging around certain friends. Part of the change came because we got new information, true, but a lot of it came from the fact that the people we were with saw certain ideas as being more important than others. We began to see perhaps that the war and the draft system were significant issues, or perhaps that we should be concerned about the Communist Party. Along with this, we began to realize that freedom or democracy or whatever might be worth working for. The example is political, but it could be in any number of areas — religious, social, economic.

The power of environments over us is greater than we usually suppose. Often we have a hard time holding out against them, even when we disagree. Young Catholics frequently go through this experience in high school, at universities or in military service. They are taught to believe that Christ is important and that certain sexual values are correct. Then they find themselves in the middle of environments in which the opposite is the common opinion (sometimes explicitly or sometimes simply because certain other values are held, like the overriding importance of money or status). Then they find themselves gradually tending to think in ways that presuppose Christ is not important, even though inside somewhere, they still think he is. Or they find themselves adopting certain sexual values or ways of acting, even though they feel guilty about them and, put in the right situation (a retreat, for instance), would readily accept the fact that they are wrong.

Not every environment, it is true, has a strong effect on a person's life. If a person does not like a situation he is in or the people in it, he will be much less affected by it. Or if the environment is a weak one, that is, if the people have a low degree of interest in each other and in the situation as a whole and there is not much vitality to it, the people in it will not be very much affected by it (this is one reason why being in certain classes in school can have so little effect on the students or why often people are very little changed by their work environments). Or if a person has a strong environment in his life counteracting another environment (say, if he belongs to a strong religious group that counteracts the effect of being in an environment in which certain kinds of immorality or disbelief are accepted), he will not be as much affected by that environment. But, if a person does not have any environment in his life which is favoring something, he will have a hard time keeping that thing as part of his life.

What I have been saying is that we depend on others for our beliefs, for what we think is important, for the ways in which we act. We take these things from those around us to a great degree. This is not bad. If someone had to think everything out for himself and decide upon everything himself, he would make very slow progress. He might reach the level of a caveman if he were fortunate. It is good that we are affected by our environments, but that only points up the need to realize the kind of effect that environments can have upon us.

In many ways we do. Instinctively, we know enough not to hang around with certain people if we want to keep our moral standards. And when we decide that we want to have something new in our lives (perhaps we want to become better Christians, or perhaps we want to develop new human relationships), we instinctively look for human beings who live the way we want to live or who can do the kinds of things we want to be able to do. We know we will pick up the new thing a lot easier by being a part of a group than by trying to "go it alone."

Since environments are so important in human life, it is necessary to take them into account in pastoral work. This has been done to some degree in the past. Much effort has been expended in trying to keep Catholic students away from secular schools and to keep Catholics away from the YMCA and other environments which are not "Catholic." This effort made a certain degree of sense (given the fact that we wanted to keep people Catholic), but it was largely negative. The effort was to keep people out of "bad" environments.

While it still may be important to keep people out of "bad" environments (though it is becoming harder and harder to do so in a world of such mobility and communications), it is much more important to provide people with the environments which will make it possible for them to live as Christians even if they have to be part of "bad" environments. This is primarily what is meant by taking environments into account in pastoral work. If a person is going to live as a Christian with very much vitality, it is necessary for him to be a part of a Christian environment. That does not mean that every environment in his life has to be Christian. But it does mean that some (at least one) environments in his life have to be Christian, and providing such environments should be one of the major tasks of any pastoral efforts.

In order to understand what it might mean to say

that a person needs to be part of an environment that is Christian, it is necessary to have a clear idea of what a "Christian environment" is. The most common misconception in this area is that if all the people are Christian then the environment is Christian too: If a school (or college or Newman Center or neighborhood or club, etc.) is made up of all Catholics, it is a Catholic school. But to say this is to misunderstand how an environment functions. Take the example of a corner tavern. Everyone who frequents that tavern may actually be fairly patriotic. But it would be a mistake to automatically assume, therefore, that the atmosphere of the tavern is patriotic or that it fosters patriotism. It might, but it might not. More likely what is fostered at that tavern is, say, sports or sex, or whatever else people focus on when they are there. Patriotism may never enter into the patron's interaction at all.

In other words, the kind of environment a particular environment is depends on how the people interact. If the people in a group are all patriots and yet never talk about it or indicate that it is important to them in any way, that environment is not patriotic and it does not foster patriotism. It may not be an antipatriotic environment, and so it may not work against patriotism, but it is not "a patriotic environment."

The realization that a Christian environment is more than an environment composed of Christians reveals a serious deficiency in the previous pastoral approach of the Church. It has often been assumed that simply being in a group that was all Catholic would be enough to make a person a good Catholic. Being in an all-Catholic group may have helped in the sense that the people in Catholic schools, for instance, usually were not against Catholicism or against Christian values, unlike people in some other environments. But very often Catholicism or Christianity was not fostered in the all-Catholic group. It was not a Christian environment, even though everyone in it was a Christian.

For an environment to be a Christian environment, Christianity has to be part of the way people in that environment interact. They have to talk about it in a way that shows that they consider it important and accept it. They have to do things which show that it is of value to them (or let people know that they do these things). People have to be not only Christian, but it has to be clear to the others that they are Christian, and the environment as a whole has to accept Christianity (not, of course, that every single person in it has to be Christian or accept Christianity any more than everyone at a university has to be liberal for it to be a liberal environment).

For many people in the Church today, the only really Christian environment they have experienced was a Christian family (although many have not even experienced that). In some families, it is still the practice for the parents to talk to each other and to the children about Christ and the importance of following him. They pray together, go to Mass together, sometimes even read parts of scripture or some Christian book together and discuss it. Christianity is a part of the way they interact, the basis of it. Such families are, however, getting rarer and rarer. Even rectories and convents are often not Christian environments in this sense (they are only Christian environments in the sense that everyone in them is engaged in Church work, but often there is no *personal,* that is, free, voluntary, and spontaneous interaction that centers on Christ).

Here is a major problem which the Church faces. A Christian must have an environment in his life in which Christianity is openly accepted, talked about, and lived if he is going to be able to live a very vital Christian life. If he does not have this, his whole life as a Christian will be weak and might even die away. Yet fewer and fewer Catholics are finding such an environment.

ENVIRONMENTAL AND INSTITUTIONAL APPROACHES

2) Environmental factors are more basic than institutional factors in Christian growth and therefore the primary pastoral concern should be in forming Christian environments rather than reforming Christian institutions.

Today when people consider pastoral action, their primary concern seems to be to change institutions. In the parish, for example, they think immediately of starting a parish council or getting a social action organization going or beginning a parent-educator program. This kind of change is valuable, but it is not so important as providing a Christian environment — and it is not the same thing as providing a Christian environment.

An institution is a stable pattern of human interrelationship which is designed (or has evolved) to get some job done. General Motors Corporation is an institution, as is the city government, or a boy scout troop. Schools, businesses, parishes, political parties are all institutions. They are groupings of human beings

33

which work together to get something accomplished.

Although institutions and environments often go together, there is a difference between institutions and environments. They are distinct patterns of human interrelationship with different laws governing them. An institution exists for the sake of some job. It is task-oriented or accomplishment-oriented. Environments do not "do" anything. They are relationship-oriented. They exist because people want to be together with other people. Or to be more accurate, environments exist because people *need to* be together with other people in order to function well.

The main relationships in an institution are work relationships and they tend to be functional. The relationships in an environment are personal. People relate more directly as people and less according to a function they are performing. The basis of their relationship might be a common ideal or a common interest, but it is not a common job. That does not mean that there cannot be jobs or task-oriented work together on things, and there are jobs that members of families have to do, but these things are not the basis of their being together.

Environmental relationships and institutional relationships often exist in the same human groupings. For instance, the university is an institution, but there is also an accompanying environment. Insofar as the university is an organized system for educating people it is an institution. Because there is also a pattern of relationships among people who have come together, there is a university environment. Many activities that go on in the university environment are virtually untouched by the university as an institution (the drug traffic, for instance). Some of the most important factors in the university as an institution exist in little or no connection with the university environment (the board of trustees, or the legislature sometimes). In short, even when institutions and environments go together, they are still distinct.

Sometimes environments and institutions exist apart from one another. Some environments exist without an institution. Groups of friends can be strong environments which are sometimes fairly large and do not have institutions which bring them into existence as a group or maintain their life as a group. Some institutions exist without an environment. There is a mail order firm which sells pamphlets that is made up of people who do not work together and hence have only institutional relations. But it is rare to find an institution that either does not have an environment or does not function within one.

A social grouping could be described as an institution when the institutional factors predominate, an environment when the environmental factors predominate. For instance, a business corporation like GM is primarily an institution. It is an organization that is formed to perform an economic function. The people come together because of it, and no one is part of it who does not have an institutional function in its operations. There are a variety of environments in GM (groups of friends, for example), but they are not the primary factor in the grouping we call GM. A social club, on the other hand, is primarily environmental. It exists so that the members can get together and socialize. It is an institution too, but the institutional part of it exists only to further the environmental interrelationship. The university, however, is in between. There are a great many people in the university environment (this varies, of course, from university to university) who are not part of the university as an institution, and many things happen within the university environment which are not related to the university as an institution (political groups, cultural groups, etc.). But the university does have a task it is trying to perform beyond just forming and servicing an environment. It is an organization which offers educational services.

Families and communities are environments, not institutions. According to some definitions, the family is an institution in society, but not according to the one given above. Sometimes it can be hard to tell whether a particular grouping is an environment or an institution. A parish, for instance, can be a real community, that is, an environment. Or it can be simply an institution, a religious organization providing certain services to its members.

A person can be a part of an institution in a variety of ways. He can be forced into it (a prisoner or slave is) or paid (workers usually are at their jobs mainly for this reason) or he can choose it (volunteer organizations exist on this basis). But a person can be a part of an environment only by being willing to be. A person can be forced by circumstances to live with a group of people, but if none of them want to have anything to do with each other, they will not form a real environment. In work situations, very often some of the workers do not take part in the environments that form among the workers, because they do not choose to. The reason environments have such an effect on their members is that the members are in some way a voluntary part of them (they want to have something to do with this particular group of people), and therefore they are open to being influenced by them. They will adopt the beliefs, attitudes, values and behavior patterns of the group so they can be part of the group. And usually the more the group means to them, the more the values they accept in this group will also be part of their lives outside the group.

Environmental factors are more basic than institutional factors in Christian growth, then, because an institution can get people to follow certain patterns of behavior but it cannot touch their basic beliefs, attitudes, and values without some sort of environmental process. The university is an academic concern, and it succeeds in getting people to perform certain academic actions (study, writing, etc.), but often it does not succeed in getting them committed to the values it is trying to foster. Usually there are environments within a university (groupings of students, for instance) in which academic concern is discouraged. Usually also, many, many students leave the university and leave behind study and all academic concern. It has not become part of their lives. It was just an activity the university demanded so that they could get a degree in order to, say, make money. If, however, students who enter the university without any academic interests find friends at the university who have a real academic concern, they will develop an academic interest, and it will probably be with them the rest of their lives.

The same thing is true of many Church institutions today. An example are religious education programs. It is generally agreed that many of the older approaches to catechism were very ineffective from the point of view of educational methods. Today, on the other hand, there are many instruction programs which are excellent from the point of view of educational methods. Yet catechism had a real impact in the Church 30 years ago and religious education has much less now. It had more impact because there was an environmental dynamic going which made people want to go along with the institutional efforts. More children came to catechism, because Catholics thought it was important, and when they came they were changed by the programs more than they are now, because the class as a whole came thinking it was important and students were ready to accept what was said (even though perhaps they were not ready to like the process involved at all). In other words, the Church today can perfectly design a program that is interesting and successful in teaching people to live as Christians, and if all the Christians live only in environments which lead them to put little value on religion (or on living as Christians), the program will be a flop. The only hope is for the religious education program to be part of a wider program to form an environment which will motivate the students to want to be Christian and to want to learn about Christianity.

Environments, on the other hand, can change people without relying on institutional helps. For instance, there has been a change in sexual morality in the United States despite the fact that there has been little institutional support for it (in fact, many institutions in

American society have been against it). The environmental dynamic has effected the change. Moreover, some of the most effective changes in Catholics have come in noninstitutional ways (the "underground churches" or Pentecostal prayer groups, for instance). These changes are not necessarily anti-institutional (some are), but they have managed to spread rapidly and change people without any institutional helps.

What we have said does not argue that institutions are not important for the growth of Christianity. But it does mean that in something like Christianity, where people are Christians not because they are paid to be or coerced to be, but because they voluntarily choose to be, institutions must be looked at in a different way than, say, in industry or government. In Christianity, institutions have to be looked at as secondary, because the primary thing which changes people (makes them Christians, makes them better or worse Christians) is the effect of environments, the free interaction of people which promotes or fails to promote Christianity. Institutions are effective only when they create or help such environments — or when they are based on such environments (like a Christian action group which draws upon an environment of real Christianity).

In other words, institutional concerns are not irrelevant to Christian renewal, but they are secondary. The primary concern has to be in forming Christian environments. Institutions which foster this process (and draw upon it) are valuable. Those which do not, are not. In fact, the whole question of how to design or evaluate a Christian institution cannot be answered except by understanding the environmental dynamic of Christianity and seeing how the institution contributes to this dynamic.

FORMING CHRISTIAN ENVIRONMENTS (COMMUNITIES)

3) When society as a whole cannot be expected to accept Christianity, then it is necessary to form communities within society to make Christian life possible.

The main goal of pastoral work is to provide Christian environments, environments within which Christianity is openly expressed and accepted, environments within which a person can find the support he needs to be a Christian. The question that remains is the question of how such environments can be formed. Our society is not Christian. Even within our churches, Christian environments are not so easy to find. What can be done?

The answer is that we need to form "Christian communities." A community is a type of environment — a strong, effective form of environment. In the next chapter the nature of "community" will be discussed, and the different meanings of the word will be distinguished. In this section, community is understood as a Christian environment.

A historical perspective provides a way of seeing more clearly the pastoral situation of the Church today as regards environmental forces and community. In the first 300 years of Christian history, the Church had a very effective form of social organization for helping Christians to live as Christians. Those who became Christians then perceived Christianity as the most important thing that ever happened to the human race. They readily joined with other Christians for the purpose of living as Christians. The communities they joined were relatively small and tightly knit, with a high degree of morale and social cohesion. The result was that a person who lived in the Christian Church in the early centuries had a great deal of help in living as a strong Christian. He was part of an environment (a community) which was much stronger than any other environment he was part of, and it provided for him a strong support in being a Christian. Because of their strength and vitality, these communities attracted other men to Christianity.

In the course of the fourth century, a major change occurred. The Roman emperors became Christians, and they made Christianity the state religion. The result was a revolution in the way Christianity was related to the environmental forces of the time. In a relatively short period, all of society became Christian (part of the Church). Christians no longer existed in strong communities within society, but being part of society and being Christian became the same thing. The Church became the religious institution for all of society and the state became the political institution for all of society. In other words, Christendom (a society almost all of whose members accepted Christianity) was formed.

Christendom brought many benefits to Christian life. For one thing, it brought many more people to the Christian faith and life. At the beginning of the fourth century, the Christians were a relatively small percentage of the Roman Empire. At the end of the fifth century, the pagans were a relatively small percentage of the Roman Empire. Every environment in society (with the

41

exception of some frontier situations where two civilizations made contact and, for a while, some remote rural situations) was Christian. There was a strong force drawing people to Christianity and keeping them Christian.

Moreover, because Christianity was the life of society, everything in life could be Christianized and directed toward the glory of God. The following centuries were times in which men tried to see all of life in a Christian way. It would be too much to say that they succeeded perfectly. But the results were impressive.

There was, however, at the same time a certain price to be paid in this change. The environment worked to make more people Christian than had been Christian before, it is true, but it also produced a lower overall level of Christianity among Christians. For one thing, since everyone was a Christian, people were not called upon to make their Christianity a matter of personal choice the way they had to when there were other options. Also, because a person had to become an outcast in society if he stopped being a Christian (since it was a Christian society), many people were inclined to stay Christians even though they had no desire to live a Christian life while before they would have just dropped out. Also, it became harder to maintain Church discipline when the Church was no longer a tightly knit community within society from which someone could be easily excluded.

In the course of the 17th and 18th centuries, another revolution occurred in the way Christianity was related to the environmental forces of the time. Society began to fall away from Christian belief. It became acceptable in society not to believe in Christianity (it was socially acceptable even before it was legally acceptable). The change began among certain thinkers in France and England who moved toward deism and a skepticism about Christianity. By the 18th century, the Enlightenment, represented by men like Voltaire, Diderot, Priestly and many others, was a dominant force in Europe. Environments began to change one by one, and as environments changed, the faith of the Christian people weakened. Because they had been taught to identify "what was right" in matters of religion with "what was accepted by society as a whole" most people began to weaken in their Christian conviction and their Christian living when they saw that Christianity was not being accepted by society as a whole the way it had been.

In the Church of the first centuries, the fact that most men did not believe in Christianity was not necessarily a motive for losing faith. In fact, for many it was a strengthening motive, because they expected that when they became Christians, they were joining a group within society that had something the rest of society did not have. But since by the end of the 17th century Christians considered themselves to be society and not a group within society (they identified themselves primarily as Frenchmen or Europeans and not primarily as Christians), a change in the religious conviction of society meant a change in the religious convictions of Christians. Therefore as society became less and less supportive of a person's being a Christian, there was a gradual weakening of the environmental support most

Christians had for being Christians. For the first time in the history of the Church, the whole Church was faced with a weakening of environmental support for being a Christian.

A variety of things happened as a result of this change. Some environments in Western society stayed Christian because they were out of touch with the main currents of society (many rural environments are still in this condition today, although less and less so). In the United States, ghettos were formed by immigrants who had little social contact with the rest of the country because of the nationality difference (and this trend was strengthened by the attempts of the Church to maintain a separate school system and a separate social system, by forbidding mixed marriages, etc.). These ghettos stayed Catholic — in fact, they tended to perpetuate a form of Christendom. But in an increasing number of situations in Western society, the environment provided less and less support for thinking and living as a Christian, and the result was a weakening of Christian life.

Today many parts of Western society are de-Christianized, and the trend is in that direction. In fact, even within Church institutions, even in environments which during the 19th and the first half of the 20th centuries were traditionally Christian (like Polish or Irish neighborhoods in American cities), the environmental forces are now against Christianity. Since there is less and less of a natural separation between different environments (modern forms of communication have drawn modern society much closer and made it much more homogeneous), the Church can rely less and less on natural

44

environmental forces (rural or ghetto conservatism, for instance, or separate school systems) to maintain Christian life.

There are two pastoral approaches that can be taken in the face of the de-Christianization of Western society. One is to try to make society as a whole Christian (or different environments as a whole Christian). Traditionally this has only worked when someone or some group of people who had control over a whole environment (the secular rulers, usually) became Christian and were willing to use their influence to Christianize the parts of society they were in control of. Conceivably making environments as a whole Christian might also be accomplished through Christians and Christian ideas beginning to permeate society or different environments in society gradually, the way technological changes or political ideas begin to premeate society gradually. But the approach of making society as a whole Christian does not seem very feasible, because society as a whole is resistant to Christianity, and therefore it seems highly unlikely either that secular rulers would or could make all of society Christian or that Christianity will permeate society by natural trends.

The second pastoral approach is to form Christian communities. This approach would mean returning to the strategy which the early Church (and many other religious groups throughout the centuries) found so successful. A real Christian community (especially in a society like our own in which there is little sense of common purpose and identity) would have the ability to provide an environment in which people could live strong Christian lives. If people can find Christian communities which are alive, they will have the strength as Christians to exert an influence upon society (and not simply conform to society). And the more these Christian communities grow, the greater the effect they will have upon society.

The main goal of pastoral action in the Church today can be described in a variety of ways. We need to find an alternative form of Church life to a Christendom approach. To use a phrase which Karl Rahner made popular: We need to form a diaspora Christianity. We need to find a way of providing for people an authentically Christian environment of sufficient strength to make it possible for them to live as vital Christians if they so choose. We need to form real Christian communities.

3

A Pastoral Structure--
Basic Christian Communities

The Church should be restructured to form basic Christian communities.

That there has to be a renewal in the structure of Church life is generally accepted. But, as was discussed in the previous chapter, there is a tendency to think that structural renewal and institutional (or organizational) renewal are the same. Few people think in terms of environmental (or communal) structures. Therefore, when there is talk of structural renewal, the priorities are pastoral councils, new apostolic organizations, changes in school systems, changes in religious rules, etc. But it is rare for people to ask the basic question: How can a Christian environment (a Christian community) be formed most effectively?

The same problem can be looked at from a different point of view. The goal of the Church is not to have structures, but to have people who are living as Christians. But both the scriptures and knowledge of the way human beings function make clear that no one is complete as a Christian by himself. Christians are complete only when they belong to a full Christian community, a community in which all the things which are ordinarily needed by anyone to grow as a Christian can be provided. The basic question, then, is how to provide communities which can meet all the ordinary needs Christians have when they are living as Christians in the modern world.

The problem we are concerned with could also be considered the problem of parish renewal. In theory the parish is the basic Christian community. It is supposed to be the smallest pastoral unit in the Church, the ordinary place in which a person's Christian life can be nourished. Yet it is clear that most parishes as we know them are not such places, partly because of their size, partly because of the way they are structured. There have been a number of efforts to deal with this problem: the San Miguelito project in Panama, the community of St. Severin in Paris, the "communion" system in the Lansing, Michigan, diocese, to name only three. Often these programs of parish renewal do not focus clearly on the question of the basic community. They are, however, trying to deal with the basic problem — the problem of how to restructure Church life so that there will be a community available which can meet the needs of the Christian people, a community which will make it possible for them to be strong Christians in the modern world.

A major problem in dealing in this area is that we do not tend to think much in environmental terms or in communal terms. American life leads us to think more often in terms of organizations and task-oriented groups.

Moreover, because American business and government have so many resources available to fund research, a large proportion of the creative thinking and writing about social groupings has been done on organizations. There is a great deal in modern business administration and social sciences on organizations and how they can function. There is much less available on communities and environments and how they can be created or made to function well.

A further problem in dealing with this subject is that we do not have much experience in modern American society with communities in the sense in which this chapter is going to speak of them. We are familiar with institutions. We are familiar with communities in the sense in which cities or villages are communities, that is, units of society. We are familiar with unorganized communities, groupings of people who have a genuine voluntary unity, but who are not organized. But we have not often encountered the type of community that will be considered here — organized communities of a large size within society — and so we do not have much experience of how they function or what they are like. They exist in some Protestant sects, in some ethnic groups that have not yet been pulled apart by modern society, and in some rural situations, but they are not part of the experience of most American Catholics. Certain questions immediately arise: Why is my parish not a basic Christian community? Why are not the friends I know from CFM, the discussion group, the Cursillo, the prayer meeting, a basic Christian community? Doesn't a person have to join a religious order to belong to a Christian community? Because we have little experience with functioning communities, we do not know why other communal groupings are not basic communities or what can be done to form such communities.

To understand what it means to say that the Church should be restructured to form basic Christian communities and to understand how it might come about, it is necessary to understand:

1) what the difference is between a basic Christian community and other groupings,
2) what the structure of a basic Christian community should be like, and
3) how basic Christian communities could be formed in our present situation.

COMMUNAL STRUCTURES

This section is concerned with a certain kind of structure. Since we tend to think of structures in organizational terms, we do not readily recognize what kinds of structures environments or communities have. Even a group of friends has a structure to their common life. There are certain patterns to their interaction. They tend to meet together at certain times and places. Certain members of the group tend to have more influence on the others. These structures are not institutional or formalized, but they exist and can be recognized. Our concern in this section, then, is with communal structures — the structures which communities tend to have.

What is meant by the term "basic Christian community" is difficult to understand for two reasons. One reason has already been talked about: Americans, especially American Catholics, have no experience with "basic Christian communities." The second reason is that the word "community" is used to refer to a great variety of things. Almost every possible social grouping is called a community at one time or another. The most common groupings the word is used to refer to are:

— the parish
— unorganized communities (social environments)
— small groups (including sometimes the family)
— religious orders or congregations as a whole
— local convents or religious houses
— the diocese
— a societal group (the city, the village, the neighborhood).

None of these is what is meant by "a basic Christian community."

The parish and basic community: The present parish structure is a good place to begin in trying to understand what basic Christian communities are, because it is the most commonly experienced form of communal life in the Church today. What follows is a description and comparison of a typical parish with a Christian community. The description of the Christian community fits a number of smaller Protestant churches and a number of communities within the Catholic Church, either floating parishes or communities which center around special community Masses or prayer meetings.

The first example is that of a fairly typical Catholic parish. This parish is situated in a suburb in a large metropolitan area in the United States. There are about 1500 families in the parish. To serve these Catholics, there are six Masses on Sunday, three each weekday, a number of chances for confession, and a variety of special programs and organizations (convert instructions, a marriage program, CCD, an elementary school, the CFM, etc.). It is, in other words, a complete, modern parish.

The average parishioner in this parish comes to Mass only on Sunday. Some of his children are enrolled in the parish school, one in CCD, but these are the only parish functions anyone in the family is involved in apart from Mass and confession. When this parishioner comes to Mass, he finds himself in a Church filled with people he does not know for the most part, and who are a different group from the last group he went to Mass with the previous Sunday. The Mass he attends is "standard" for that Sunday (the Masses in this parish are fairly much identical and are little different from the Masses in other parishes that have been moderately affected by renewal). He can find out what is going to happen at Mass next Sunday (except for the content of the sermons and the announcements) by reading ahead in the missalette.

At Mass, this parishioner rarely knows the person sitting next to him unless it is a member of his own family. There is no interaction among the whole group at Mass that is not a matter of going through prearranged forms which any group of people could do with only minimal preparation. Our parishioner knows a number of other people in the parish, but he knows very few *because* they are members of the parish. He knows them because some are neighbors, some are personal friends, one is his barber, another owns a store he buys from regularly. In other words, they are people whom he happens to know from another source and who also happen to go to this parish. He does not know them because he met them through the parish. He knows very few people because of the parish, and the parish enters into his personal relationships in a very limited way.

The parish itself has a mainly organizational unity. If it were not for the mailing list and the building, the parish would be unable to make contact with the parishioners. The parish is primarily a service institution, providing Mass and sacraments for all who come to them. The leadership in the parish (the clergy) have mainly institutional ties to the parish. They are clergy because they have gone through a certain training program, met all the requirements and then were ordained. They are in that parish because they have been assigned there to fulfill certain functions. They can be replaced by any others who have been through the seminary and have been ordained.

There is another group in the parish who should be mentioned — the regulars. These are the people who come to parish affairs and who are called upon to work in various ways in the parish. They are the main source of parish activities, and they know each other because they have worked together. They are a recognizable environment, but not a very strong one (not in this parish, nor probably are their counterparts in most parishes). The average parishioner is not one of them.

The second example is that of an actually functioning Christian community. It centers around a meeting to which about 300 people come each week. Each week, it is the same group of people who come together, and therefore they can be formed into a community in an ongoing way. The average person in this community knows most of the people in the meeting by name and almost all of them by sight. Moreover, he knows them because he has met them through the community and not because he associated with them somewhere else and they just happened to be at the meeting.

Each week the meeting is different. It is responsive to the needs of the community at that time. There is a sense of development from meeting to meeting as the community develops. The person who comes feels a sense of interaction among the members of the community and a sense of identification with this particular group of people as a community. Moreover, almost all of the members of the community find themselves drawn into a number of other meetings for prayer, formation, service projects and social events, none of which involves all the members of the community, but all of which are outgrowths of the community and part of the community life. As someone becomes part of the life of the community, he is drawn into service of others in the community.

The body of the people and their gathering together is the focus of this community, not the mailing list or the building (the latter they do not have). It is possible to "pass the word around" and reach everyone in the community. Every member of the community is an active participant. There are few people there just to receive religious services. The organizational aspect of the community is organic — it is developed to meet needs the community feels, not to supply services the community ought to want. The leadership within this community is a "natural" or "emergent" leadership; that is, within the process of organic growth in the community certain people emerged as being "naturals" to fulfill certain functions within the community. They were the ones the community wanted to have lead them. There is a priest in the leadership, but he chose the community and the community chose him. He was not assigned to the community. He was chosen because the community could accept him as a spiritual leader.

The parish and the Christian community just described are two quite different community structures. The parish was primarily developed in a Christendom situation. It is an institution which has been developed to provide certain religious services to a society (an environment) which is Catholic. It was successful so long as society motivated people to want to be Catholics and to want the services of the parish. In an ethnic neighborhood or a small town, there was quite a bit of community connected with the parish — it was the center of a real environment. But in the modern city or suburban parish, this is less and less the case. In fact, in the parish described, it would be hard to tell whether it should be considered a communal structure or an institutional structure which provides certain religious services, because there is almost no personal interaction among the average parishioners; there is less than there is among the employees in a business corporation, in fact. There are, of course, all kinds of parishes and some may be more or less genuine Christian communities. The example picked was of a common type of parish which is more a religious institution than a community. It was used to show the difference between a grouping which is often referred to as a community, but could be better described as a service institution or a religious institution.

The Christian community we described is a cohesive environment. It has a great deal of vitality because it is a real community. It is primarily based on personal relationships (the relationships the members have to this body of people) rather than on programs or activities (services). It centers around a gathering of the community which forms one community in a strong, visible way. Its structure is based on the natural structure of communal interrelationships and on emergent leadership, not on a primarily institutional structure and on a leadership which is there by assignment and is acceptable primarily because of a course of training and a status. In other words, a basic Christian community is quite different from a parish structure as many people know it.

Unorganized and basic community: There is another communal structure in the Church today which is what many people think of when they think of "community." It is not as common as the parish structure, but it is still more common to have community in this sense than to have a basic Christian community. This structure is the unorganized community (the social environment).

The unorganized community has come about fairly commonly in the Church today as a result of the changes in the modern Church. Many movements in the Church have given rise to community in this sense: the liturgical movement, social action movements, CFM, the Cursillo, the Charismatic Renewal. "Unorganized community" refers to a group of people who are bound together by the same ideals and values, and who know one another, but who do not have a formal organization or structure. They make contact with one another because they frequent the same activities. They gravitate toward each other because they hold the same ideals, but they have no more structure than a social environment might, a group of friends, perhaps.

A good way to get hold of what is meant by an "unorganized community" is to follow the description of an actual community of its kind which existed six years ago and now exists only in an attenuated form. This particular community got its start in the wake of Vatican II when much of renewal was still unpopular among most laymen and priests. The "community" was formed in a small city among laymen (and some order priests) who were "liberals." The original catalyst for the group was a "dialogue Mass" (in those days, that meant a Mass at which you could respond in Latin) begun by a priest influenced by the liturgical movement. Later catalysts were CFM and the Cursillo movement. It was a group drawn together by interest in liturgy, community, the apostolate (mainly social action projects) and various forms of renewal.

When it was thriving, the group was drawn together because of common values. The various members identified with one another as having something important in common. They had met at certain functions ("liturgical" Masses, Cursillos, CFM groups and study days) and gotten to know each other. Even a parish Mass or just a party would provide them contact at which they could meet and talk about the things held in common.

It was quite clear when someone was really in this group, and it was clear enough that most Catholic laymen and priests were not. Yet there was no formal membership, no meeting of the group. An average "member" would know a number of others in the community, but he would not know most of them. Yet he would feel a sense of camaraderie with them all and would find it easy to develop some kind of relationship with other members when he met them.

There was no organization to this community. It arose by a natural process. It was fed by certain organized programs — in fact, it gave rise to most of these programs. But it was not organized as a community. As a result a great part of the Christian needs of the group had to be met outside the "community." The parish provided most of these — Mass regularly, basic religious education, marriage, etc. The community itself could not meet any of these needs (and, of course, the fact that the "members" had to participate in activities led by people of quite different ideals and interests caused a certain amount of frustration). There was a certain kind of leadership in the community. Some people were known especially for setting direction, people who thought creatively and acted upon the ideas which were part of the life of the community. But these leaders were only leaders by example, not by having an accepted role within the community.

This community no longer exists. It has descendants. There is an "underground church" which has come from this community, and it has much the same structure as this community did. There are a number of other "unorganized communities," each one centering about a particular concern — social action, prayer, sensitivity training — which are also descendants of this original community.

The difference between such a community and a basic Christian community of the type described above is the organization that belongs to the basic Christian community. The basic community is primarily an environment, but it also has enough organization to be able to function. It can meet the religious needs of its members, because it can act. Its members are not dependent upon organizations not made up of members of the community for their basic needs. Moreover, because it is organized, it has a gathering at which the community can meet and be formed and developed. Its leadership is made up of people who have a natural "authority" within the group, but who also have an accepted role within the community. They lead not only by natural influence, but they also do some of the work which goes into meeting the needs of the community. Or, to put it another way, the basic Christian community is both an environment and an institution, not just an environment like the unorganized community is. The institution is something which is an outgrowth of the dynamics of the community and not something which is there for people to take part in if they want to or not. Neither the environment nor the institution exists outside the other. Each supports the other.

There is a great strength to the "unorganized community." It has strength as an environment, because it is completely voluntary. It avoids all the dangers of institutionalism. There is no bureaucracy, no inhibiting procedures or the dead weight of worthless structures.

But there is also a great weakness to it. It is completely at the mercy of environmental forces. The community described above dissipated after the initial enthusiasm over Vatican II waned and "the liberal camp" began to splinter. Because there was no organization to it, it could not find a way to maintain a unity or to deal with the problems posed to its "program" by the new circumstances. Most of the members regretted the fact that "the community" no longer existed, but they could not do anything about it.

A basic community, then, is not the same as an unorganized community. There are many types of informal community in the Church today, but none of these actually forms a basic community. A basic community is more like an organism. It has a certain amount of organization. It can function as a unity. It can act. Moreover, there is a certain amount of commitment involved in belonging to it. Those who belong to it take part in its life regularly, not just when they feel like it. They support it in a regular way and therefore make more things possible in the life of the community.

Small groups and basic community: There is still another type of communal structure in the Church today which many people think of when they hear the word "community": the small group. "Small groups" as used here means only permanent or semipermanent groups that are a regular part of the life of the Church. These small groups include discussion groups, prayer groups, action groups, group reunions, and groups that live together (most commonly groups of priests, brothers, and nuns or families). These groups have a regular existence which meets some needs in the life of the Church in an ongoing way. We are not here concerned with the discussion group after a talk, the ad-hoc committee, the short-term action group — groups which get together for a specific, temporary purpose.

There are a variety of reasons for having small groups. The first one is to provide primary relationships among Christians. In a small group, Christians can get to know one another in a personal way. There is a warmth and an individuality of relationship that cannot exist in a larger group. Everyone is known there, and if one person is missing, the rest of the group realizes it. Each person within the group has spoken to everyone else and is familiar with all. There is a need for this kind of relationship in the Christian life: being able to talk regularly with a few people about Christianity.

There is a need for primary relationships among members of a community if the community and its life are going to mean very much to the people involved. It is usually only when a person encounters an environment in a face-to-face relationship with someone else that it begins to change him. Moreover, it is in personal sharing and talking about the common ideal (in this case, Christianity) that a person learns most quickly and grows toward it.

A further reason for having small groups is that they provide a place for individual needs to be met. The life of a community is weak if each person does not have a place in which he can express himself personally, get individual attention, and be of help to others. Large meetings cannot allow for adequate individual help.

Finally, small groups can provide ways of accomplishing things the whole community cannot accomplish in any other way. There is a need for small groups to work together to get jobs done. There is a need for small groups to meet together to learn. There is a need for small groups to meet together for different kinds of prayer or sharing. There are certain things all the members of a community need at the same time. There are other things that should be taken care of in smaller groupings.

There is a certain tendency to look only for small groups when looking for community. Many proposals for the renewal of parish life (or for the renewal of life in the different Protestant congregations) rely mainly on providing small groups for everyone in the parish. The thought seems to be that if there are small groups for everyone, that will take care of providing the environmental support which is needed to make the parish structure viable. There is a great deal to be said for the small group approach. Every Christian community, if it is going to be very successful, has to provide small groups for its members. But there is a deficiency to any approach which makes use of only small groups or puts the main emphasis on the formation of small groups. Small groups by themselves are not enough.

Something more than small groups is needed, because small groups need to be part of a larger community if they are going to be able to function very long. A larger community provides stimulation for the small group. The small group that tries to get by on its own resources tends to stagnate after a while. A larger community provides balance. Small groups can tend to go off in one direction or overemphasize different things if they are not in regular communication with other groupings. A larger community provides breadth. Small groups can easily become ingrown and narrow if they are not part of a larger community.

In an approach that relies only on small groups, small groups are left to their own resources. Within a larger community, the members can get a great deal of help, much of it that will help the small group itself to function better. Sometimes the help comes from services that are available like instruction, counseling, action projects. Sometimes the help comes from personal contacts with other Christians who are not members of the small group—advice, encouragement, friendship. Sometimes the help comes from people outside the small group who are in a position to help the members of the group form well, or in a position to help them resolve conflicts or difficulties.

Small groups can be more flexible when they are part of a larger community. There is a great deal of pressure on a small group that exists by itself, a pressure that does not exist when it functions in the context of a larger community. When a group is going it alone, the success of the group is crucial for the success of the whole effort. If the group is part of a larger community, it is always possible to regroup or to find support from outside the group as well as inside the group. When they are part of a larger community as well, the members of a small group can have a more relaxed attitude to this particular group, and they do not have a tendency to make as much of a demand on the other members of the group. Consequently, personality clash is much less of a problem when a small group exists in the context of a larger community than when it exists by itself.

When a small group exists by itself, it has to do the whole job of holding people together. It has to, in effect, do most of what a community can do if its life as a group is to be very successful. The small group has to provide a common ideal and vision, a common understanding of the Christian life, a common understanding about personal relationships and how the members of the group should relate to one another. If the members of the small group are also members of a community in which people have formed a common vision of the Christian life and an understanding of how to live it, they will not have to do as much to make the small group successful as they would if they were not part of a larger community.

There is another deficiency in the approach which makes use of only small groups — it fails to appreciate that the primary relationship is not the only personal relationship Christians can have or need. There is a common misconception that the only *real* personal relationships are the kind that are formed individually or in small groups where people can "get to know each other well." According to this view, the alternatives to such relationships are functional relationships which are distant and impersonal. But this view is not really accurate. There is a definite kind of relationship that can exist among members of a real community. There is a bond that comes from having something in common, depending upon one another, living for one another — belonging to the same body. It is a bond that can exist without knowing each other well, without being tied to just a small group.

A Pastoral Structure

A different dynamic begins to develop when a group gets large enough (it usually begins about 30-40), a dynamic which makes certain kinds of things possible which are not possible in a smaller group. A large group that is united, of one mind and of one heart, has a strong effect upon people. In addition, a social grouping has a certain vitality when the members are less homogenous and more diverse (whereas great diversity often makes it difficult for a small group to function well), when all different types are represented and brought together. A large group can provide a breadth to the common life and experience which the small group cannot (although the smaller group can find a depth that the larger group cannot). In other words, something happens when human beings form larger groupings which cannot happen in small groups and vice versa.

What has been said about small groups throws light upon another area of Christian life—households. Households, whether families or religious houses, are small groups. They are small groups that live together and so are distinct from other small groups, but they are nonetheless small groups. Consequently, they have need of being part of a larger community which supports them and which they can support. In an age in which Christian family life and religious community life is breaking down, it becomes all the more crucial to realize the role of a community in the stability of households.

There is a tendency among Christians in responding to the breakdown of family life to stress the importance of the family unit itself. They tend to romanticize the husband-wife relationship and the parent-child relationship. They tend to recommend, as a solution to relation-

65

ship problems, married couples doing as much as possible together and families spending as much time together as possible. In a society with a great deal of fragmentation and in a Church without much community life, that advice is not bad advice. There is definitely a need to strengthen family life.

But Christian communities provide an alternate approach — one that can work for many more families. The common "family life emphasis" approach amounts to recommending to families that they be Christian communities. Because there is nothing else in society to hold the members of the family together, the life of the family together has to do it. But if families exist within a Christian community, they can rely on the support of the community to provide a context within which stable family life can succeed. Most families run into the problem of most small groups — they cannot go it alone for very long, especially when the children get older or the interests of the husband and wife change. Families need to be part of communities, and not just islands by themselves.

Other communal groups: There are other candidates for the use of the term "community." The diocese, the religious order or congregation, and societal groupings are often each referred to as a community (or sometimes as "the community"). For the sake of clarity, it is important to understand what the difference is between these groupings and a basic Christian community.

Technically, the diocese is the local Church. Only a diocese is a complete Christian community, because only the diocese is presided over by the bishop and he is the only one with the fullness of priestly authority. Priests (presbyters) cannot function independently of their bishop and cannot meet all the needs of their people (the conferring of Confirmation and Orders, for instance, is ordinarily reserved for the bishop).

Even though technically the diocese is the full Christian community, functionally it is not a community. The technical (canonical) view is left over from the time when the diocese was smaller and was "pastored" as a unit by the bishop. The bishop's flock were the Christians in one city and the surrounding countryside. None of the cities in the ancient world came close to the size of "small" American cities, so the "dioceses" then could not be compared to ours today.

The diocese today is no longer a local grouping. It is a regional grouping. It cannot function like a local Christian community. It cannot be a body. It cannot meet the daily needs of the Christian people. That is not to say that the diocesan (regional) groupings of Christians are not important. They are especially important today when people are more interdependent over a larger area and when more resources are needed to do certain basic things. What kind of structure the Church should have in a larger area is an important question. But for the purposes of this book, it is important only to see that a diocese is not a basic Christian community even though canonically it may be "the local church."

Nor is the religious order or congregation a basic Christian community. Frequently nuns or brothers or order priests will refer to their religious order or congregation as "my community," but they are communities in a significantly different way from basic Christian communities. They were intended to be something different.

The religious order or congregation is not (usually) a local Christian community, because it does not try to join together all types of Christians in a locality to meet their needs to live and serve as Christians. The religious orders were intended to make it possible for Christians to form specialized households, that is, to live together with other Christians who want to follow a special pattern of life and perhaps to perform a special service within the Church. The order or congregation as a whole is a support system for households that either exist on their own or in a variety of different local church situations. Some religious orders were intended to be basic Christian communities. The monastic movement began that way, and many monasteries today function as basic Christian communities. But, in general, religious orders and congregations are systems of specialized households, not local communities.

Understanding religious orders and congregations as households, not as local communities, can be a help to understanding some of their problems today. Like families, religious communities develop difficulties when they try to exist by themselves. But for the purpose of this book, it is important only to understand the difference between what is meant by "basic Christian communities" and "religious communities."

Finally, societal groupings are also often referred to as "the community." Many people, Christians included, refer to the city, the village, or society as a whole as "the community." A societal grouping, however, is significantly different from a basic Christian community, and this difference points up more clearly what is meant by "basic Christian community."

Societal groupings are, first of all, not Christian. Sometimes people have a difficult time distinguishing between societal groupings and Christian communities, because they do not have a very concrete notion of what it takes to be a Christian, and so they cannot distinguish between those who are Christians and those who are not. All men or "all men of good will" are in some way considered to be Christians. Taking this approach is fatal to the development of Christian community and Christian life — as will be discussed in the next chapter.

But societal groupings are also not communities in the same sense as basic Christian communities. Basic Christian communities are voluntary, societal groupings are not. People are born into societal groupings and are compelled to be part of them in order to survive. Elementary survival and law are the basis of the unity of societal groupings. Basic Christian communities have to be freely chosen. People are part of them because they have decided to be Christians. There was a time when this was not so true, because there were societies based on Christianity. But today it is increasingly true. And because basic Christian communities are voluntary, their source of unity is especially crucial. This too will be discussed in the next chapter.

WHAT A BASIC CHRISTIAN COMMUNITY IS

So far the basic Christian community has been treated from the point of view of what it is not. It is not a parish, it is not an unorganized community, it is not a small group, religious community, diocese or societal grouping. Now is the time to try a definition of a basic Christian community.

A basic Christian community is an environment of Christians which can provide for the basic needs of its members to live the Christian life. As such it is the smallest self-sustaining unit of Christian living. In it, its members can find on a regular basis all they need for living the Christian life.

In the definition, the term which is most vague is "the basic needs." We have gained some idea of what these basic needs are in what has been said in the last two chapters, especially in terms of personal relationships. A social grouping which can meet all the basic needs a person has in order to be able to live as a Christian has the following characteristics:

— It must be Christian: Christianity must be accepted in an open way by those in the grouping and it must be the openly accepted basis of everything that is done in it.
— It must be an environment: There must be interaction between the people in the social grouping that is personal, that is, relationship-oriented and not just task-oriented.
— It must be organized: In order for the grouping to meet the needs of its members, it must have enough organization for the members to be able to work together in service.
— It must be large enough: It must be larger than a small group, both because of the need to have a larger grouping and because there are not enough resources in a small group.

— It must be local: The members have to be close enough to one another to be in regular contact, so that the grouping can meet their regular needs to live as Christians.

— It must be complete: It cannot be a specialized community, but it must be concerned with all of what is involved in being a Christian.

— It must have a unity: There must be a basis for the life of the community which is enough to hold everyone together. The basis must be Jesus Christ, if the community is going to be a Christian community.

Each of these points brings up a number of questions. The previous chapter considered what a Christian environment is. The rest of this chapter will consider structural questions ("large enough," "local," "complete") and what is involved in them. The next chapter will discuss what it means to be an environment with a Christian unity. The fifth chapter will discuss what kind of organization a community has to have to be a community.

At the end of this book, the term "basic needs" will be clearer, but it will still not be completely defined. To do so would be to go beyond the limits of the book whose purpose is to point to the kind of communities we must have in order to meet the pastoral needs the Church is facing today. Neither is the book a complete description of what Christian community life is, nor a manual on how to form a community. To answer all the questions involved in these considerations would take us beyond what can be done well in this book.

THE STRUCTURE OF A BASIC COMMUNITY

There are many structural principles that go into forming basic Christian communities. In this section we will consider four factors (size, meetings, completeness and totality) and the principles involved in them. These questions have been selected because they make more concrete what is involved in forming basic Christian communities.

Size: The question of size is a crucial one for Christian communities. Different things happen with different sizes. Moreover, there are some limitations on the size of a community. It cannot be too small and be a real community. Nor can it be too separated geographically or kept together in too large a grouping and still maintain the oneness that belongs to a community.

First of all, there is a lower limit. If there is going to be a real community dynamic and not just a small-group dynamic, the community should be large enough. It takes a certain number of people for the kind of vitality which comes from a large group of people with real differences in personality and circumstances who are united in a common dedication.

The point at which a small group ends and a community begins is difficult to define, but it seems to happen somewhere between 20 and 40 people (depending upon the situation). In a group of 20 people, it is still possible for everyone to know everyone else in some depth. It is possible for one person to have spoken individually to all the others every week or two. In a group of 40, it is difficult for this to happen. It is not an accident that in many groups within the Church (groups of parish regulars, apostolic organizations, CYOs, Newman centers), the people who are really involved total around 30 (no matter what the size of the parish, the university, or whatever the source group might be). This size group can be held together by personal acquaintance and sharing, even if there is no leadership that knows how to form a community. It is also not an accident that when a group which has been held together by informal relationships begins to grow larger than this, there is often a crisis. People begin to say, "We aren't a community any longer," and what they mean is that they can no longer know all the people in the group and relate to them in a primary way. In other words, by the time a group reaches 40 people, it can begin to have a real community dynamic in the sense in which we have been talking about, but that ends the previous kind of small-group dynamic.

There is another factor which indicates the need for a larger size (over 40 people) for a community: the impossibility of meeting all the basic Christian needs in the community with only a small number of people to draw from. There has to be a large enough group to provide the kind of leadership which can meet the needs of the community and to support the kinds of activities which it takes to meet these needs. It would be rare for a community under 40 to be able to do this.

There are also limitations on the largeness of a community. It would not be totally correct to say that there is an upper limit to the number of people who can be in one community, but there are different kinds of limitations which indicate that it does not work simply to absorb everyone who comes. Growth in numbers can destroy a community's unity.

In order to understand the factors governing the largeness of communities, it is necessary to understand subgroupings within a community. A community can get quite large and still be one community, but it cannot get very large and still be one community without forming subgroupings. If it does, in the process it will cease to be a community. In a large amorphous community, people lose all sense of being a community.

Within a large community, there have to be what could be called basic pastoral units. The basic pastoral units have to be small enough so that everyone in the basic pastoral unit can be adequately tied into the community as a whole. There seem to be a number of factors which go into determining how large such a unit can be. Some basic pastoral units seem to have difficulty when they grow larger than 100. Others seem to function well with over 1000. A personal guess is that the normal size would be under 500.

One of the limiting factors in the size of a basic pastoral unit is the ability to have one meeting of the whole grouping. It is difficult to form a basic pastoral unit without having the whole group meet together. If the largest facility that can be found has a capacity for only 80, it is probably impossible for that community to have a basic pastoral unit over 80. A second factor is the composition of the group. A community made up of families (rather than one made up of mainly single people) can have a larger membership and still keep a unity as a community (but at the same time having a smaller adult membership).

A third limiting factor is the structure of the group.

The better a group is structured, the larger it can be and still do well as a basic pastoral unit. If a community has an inadequate small-group structure, it has to remain smaller. If the members have only an informal or limited commitment to the community, the community has to remain small. If the leadership works effectively and is structured well, the grouping can be larger. If the community is cohesive and alive, the grouping can be larger.

There is also a limiting factor on the size of the community as a whole if it is going to be considered a local community. A community can comprise all the people in a locality and still be one community no matter how many people there are so long as those people are formed into the right kind of subgroupings (basic pastoral units, small groups, etc.). But there is a limit on how large an area can be considered a locality. If it is impossible for members of the various subgroupings to meet regularly, especially the pastoral workers in the subgroupings, the community is too large to be a local community.

There is no automatic upper limit of size beyond which a community is too large to still be a community. The strength of people's ties and commitment to the community and the strength of their bond of unity with the community do not depend on the size of the community. They depend on how well the subgroupings of which they are a part function. If a person finds a good place in a subgrouping that functions well and is properly related to the community as a whole, his loyalty to the community as a whole will be very strong.

The principles we have been considering are the

principles that originally went into the formation of dioceses and parishes. The diocese is meant to be the local Christian community and the parish is meant to be the basic pastoral unit. But as the social dynamics of modern society changed, the diocese became not a local Christian community, but a regional Christian community, and the parishes became too large to be basic pastoral units. They had to become service institutions. Basic Christian communities (local Christian communities) have to be structured in a different way from the way the Church is structured today.

When we have been talking about size, we have been talking about factors of group dynamics. When groups of people are in certain sizes, they can interact only in certain ways. As a group grows, some things become possible, others impossible. It is a matter of experimentation and research, not of dogma. All groups, not just Christian ones, have to cope with these facts. Because of the rapid population growth, units that were once "community-sized" are no longer small enough. Because the Church until recently did not have to provide a Christian environment for its members, it was not forced into a consideration of this kind of group dynamics.

Meetings: In order to keep a group of, say, 200 people together as a real community, there has to be a certain structure to the life of the community. By "the structure of the life of the community" is not meant the organization of the community; that will be considered in a later section. Rather, what is meant is the regular patterns by which the people in the community get together and

76

form a common life. Under this heading, the most significant factor is meetings, because these are the regular, ongoing ways in which the community is built up and held together.

First of all, the community (the basic pastoral unit) needs a common meeting. It is very difficult for a community to actually be formed as one community without assembling together regularly. It could almost be said that it is the coming together that makes them one community. Since we are concerned with Christian communities, the common meeting is a meeting in which the community comes together with God. The center of the meeting is the worship of God, and it involves the proclamation and teaching of the word of God (scriptures) and ordinarily the Eucharist. Or, to put it another way, the liturgy should be the meeting of a community which comes together to be formed into the body of Christ. It is not meant to be primarily a service at which the people who decide to attend that particular meeting get some personal spiritual help (although that should certainly be one of the things that happen at the gathering of the community).

One of the themes of the liturgical movement was the theology of the Christian assembly. It was long recognized that the Mass was meant to be a Christian assembly. One of the earlier practices which the liturgical movement promoted in order to realize this theology was designating one of the Masses on Sunday as the parish Mass. But this was only a hesitant step toward understanding what a Christian assembly is. Unless there is a Christian community which is small enough to gather as a whole, there cannot be a real Christian assembly, because the Christian assembly is the actual assembling of a Christian community to be formed into a body of Christ. Unless a community gathers as a whole, there is no real assembly.

Besides a common meeting of the basic pastoral unit, a Christian community needs small groupings in which people can find primary personal relationships with other members of the community and can have their own needs met. A community which tries to exist with only one large meeting will not succeed very well in maintaining a vital common life. One large meeting does not allow a chance for many of the individual's needs to be met, and it does not allow a chance for the closer relationships which cement the individual's bonds with the community (if an individual does not have some people in the community to whom he is personally important, he will not feel that he is important to the community at all). In other words, a basic Christian community must have subgroupings along with its overall unity.

In order for all this to happen, a basic Christian community needs leadership which can keep it together and form it into a unity. The question of leadership will be considered further on in more detail, but what we have sketched so far has some immediate implications for the kind of leadership a Christian community needs. A pastor of a basic Christian community is going to have a different job from that of a pastor of a parish like we have now.

The pastor of the present parish has the primary task of maintaining an organizational unity for the whole parish and to see that certain slots are filled in certain activities (to see, for instance, that there is some priest at every Mass). Whether he serves 200 or 2000 people does not make that much difference. All the size difference means is that he needs more assistants to handle the greater number of Masses (if the church seats 500, he can fill it four or five times and not be overworked), confessions, and marriages.

The pastor of a basic pastoral unit of a local Christian community, however, has to know all the people and be in touch with all their needs. He has to do more than just provide some services for them. He has to keep in contact with them all. He would have a difficult time being pastor of more than 500, and he would need an assistant or two (at least part time) for even 500. In other words, the need to form basic Christian communities indicates both the need for a new way for clergy to function and also for many more of them.

Completeness: If a community is going to be a basic Christian community, it cannot be only a specialized Christian community. Communities can specialize in a variety of ways: services (a community of people dedicated to catechetical teaching), a pattern of life (monastic communities, communities designed for professional men), or political ideology (conservatives, radicals). There may be good reasons to have specialized communities, but they are different from a basic Christian community. A basic Christian community is open to all who want to be Christians in a particular locality, and it is intended to meet their needs as Christians.

It can be as difficult to specify what is involved in being "complete" as what is involved in "providing for

79

the basic needs." Being complete would certainly involve having some sort of process of bringing the people into the Christian life (a catechesis). It would involve providing a basic instruction in Christian belief and way of life. It would involve many things, but to define fully what it would mean would be to go beyond the scope of this book.

Degree of totality: Christian communities can vary a great deal in how much of the lives of the members are actually lived in common. In principle, all of a person's life belongs to the body of Christ, the Christian community he is a part of. That principle, however, can be actualized in a variety of ways.

From the point of view of degree of totality there are three main types of Christian community: the limited community, the full community, and the total community. The total community is the community in which the members of the community do everything together. A monastic community is a total community as are different communes or groups like the Amish. Because the members of a total community do everything together, their life is separated from ordinary society and from non-Christians. Communal living embraces the totality of their lives.

A second type of community is the limited community. Limited communities have only a limited area of their lives "in common." In the case of Christian communities that are limited communities, what they have in common is usually only their "spiritual life." They come together and share together their religious life. Most modern Christian groupings are limited.

The normal parish is limited. It exists solely for the religious aspect of the parishioner's life. Even a parish which has a great deal of social concern and many service projects is limited. It exists for the parishioners' religious needs and their needs for social service. Most of their lives are private in regard to the community life. Even some of the newer communities in the Church are limited. Most communities that have developed from the Cursillo movement or the Charismatic Renewal and most floating parishes are limited. They have the religious dimension of their lives (or even only part of it) in common.

The third type of community is the full community. Members of full communities have all of their lives in common, but they live in ordinary society, among non-community members. They end up doing many things apart from other members of the community, but what they do is still of concern to the community and part of the common life. Early Christian communities were full communities. When a person joined them he committed all of his life to them. His finances, for instance, were understood to be shared with the community. That does not mean that he was hired by the community or gave all of his earnings to the community (that seems to have happened only in the early Jerusalem community). But it means that he understood that the community had a claim on them, and a responsibility for the use of them and he gave as much of them as he could to the support of members of the community in need (widows, orphans, the sick). Things can be in common without having them done together with other members of the community.

There does not seem to be any reason why a basic Christian community could not be limited, full or total. As long as the community meets the basic needs of the people in it to live as Christians, it would qualify as a basic Christian community. There seems to be a question as to whether a limited Christian community will actually work in today's world, and there seems to be a trend for them to become fuller. Whether that is necessary or not, however, is difficult to answer and beyond the scope of this book.

FORMING BASIC COMMUNITIES

If we take seriously the analysis which has been made about what is needed in the Church today, there has to be a major structural change for Christianity to be able to survive in the modern world. The present parish system cannot do the job that needs to be done. It has to be replaced by many basic Christian communities. The danger that is facing us is that the Church will lose a great number of people in the near future because its structure is not adaptable to the needs of Christians in a society which does not accept Christianity. We have to get ready to undergo a major change in the structure of the Church and work to make a major change possible.

There seem to be three possible approaches to forming Christian communities. The first would be to simply draw lines across the present parish territory forming it into units of about 500 people, assign each unit a time on Sunday when they can gather together, and expect that in the place of the old parish, there would be four to five basic Christian communities formed in a year or so. This would be an unsuccessful approach to forming basic Christian communities. To take such an approach is to try to form communities by operating mainly on institutional lines. The presupposition of this approach is that forming communities is a matter of institutional restructuring. This approach (and the approach of the present parish system) is unaware of what is involved in the dynamics of environments (communities).

We are actually facing the need, not simply to reorganize the institution of the parish (although that need is certainly there), but the need to create something that is not there now—a community; that is, an environment that has a real unity to it, an organism. Organisms are not legislated. They grow naturally. In other words, an organic process of change is needed to form basic Christian communities. Cutting up the present parish system would only form smaller versions of the present parish, each without much community. It would not produce basic Christian communities. There has to be, in other words, a change in mentality. Leaders in the Church today need to understand community dynamics and not just organizational dynamics.

The second approach to forming Christian communities is the floating parish approach. This approach is to raise a flag outside the present parochial system, take the people who rally round and form them into a community. Such an approach has a lot to recommend it. When the process of forming these people into a community is done in an intelligent way, a floating parish can become a basic Christian community. But it has the disadvantage of abandoning the present parish structure, which still does have contact with many people

83

who would be completely lost to the Church if the parish structure were simply abandoned.

The third approach is the approach of trying to foster basic Christian communities within the present parishes. This approach has to begin by the recognition that the parish needs subcommunities and that these should be considered an integral part of the parish life. It should involve forming the communities in an organic way—that is, not by assigning people to form a community, but by fostering the beginnings of community among a group of people—and encouraging and guiding their growth into a basic Christian community. At the proper time, they could meet on Sunday for their community's liturgy. Eventually, as there were a number of these communities that were successful, everyone in the parish might find a place in such a community, and the parish building would be a service unit at which a number of communities might gather and it could also provide some services that basic communities might find difficult to provide out of their own resources.

This final approach is roughly the approach taken by the San Miguelito project, one of the most successful efforts today to restructure the modern Catholic parish. Reading the story of the project would help to get some concrete sense of how the process can develop ("Laymen . . . Is What It Takes!" by Francisco Bravo in *America* is an excellent description of the work of the parish), and it would also help to show how long the process can be and what a major change is needed in the attitude toward leadership in the Church.

The story of San Miguelito, however, can be misleading. San Miguelito is in an area that is theoretically all Catholic. The priests at San Miguelito were able to work among the natural groupings of people and to form them into Christian communities. In the United States, the natural social groupings would have to be converted to Catholicism, even to Christianity, before they could be formed into basic Christian communities. That means that the process has to be based, not on changing whole natural groupings, but on gathering people together into new groupings or into new environments. The task is not necessarily more difficult. It is different, however.

That the main question is not a question of structure but of a new way of people relating to one another is illustrated by many Protestant congregations. There are many Protestant churches which are structured correctly from the point of view of size, but are not communities at all. They too need to form community, even though they have a grouping that is the proper size. In many ways their situation is more difficult. It is easier to form basis Christian communities in the present Catholic parish situation, because the Catholic parish is large enough that a number of Christian communities can exist within it. It is possible to have parishioners who belong to a Christian community and parishioners who do not without their having to coexist in the same worship services and in the same activities.

It cannot, however, be emphasized too much how big a job it is going to be to form the whole Catholic Church into basic Christian communities. The change is revolutionary (although, it can only be accomplished in an evolutionary way). There has to be a major change in the mentality of the Church and of its leadership before this could happen. And along with the change in mentality, a whole new set of skills needs to be developed. Yet, characteristic of the age in which we live, there is not much time to accomplish this major change. In other words, what is needed is a commitment to an overall approach to the problems of modern Church life, a commitment to pastoral planning.

4

To What End?--
The Issue of Faith

Vital Christian communities are formed only through centering on Christ (through spiritual renewal).

In chapter two, we stated the goal of pastoral work as building Christian communities. Communities were simply defined as a type of environment. In chapter three, we considered some different ways in which environments could be structured. We sketched the kind of social grouping which is needed if Christianity is going to be able to survive in the modern world—the basic Christian community. The word "community" in this sense means an environment that is voluntary (that is, not just a societal grouping) and one which has a formal structure.

Now we have to pay some attention to that which draws the community together, that which gives it unity. A voluntary grouping within society can exist only if it has a source of unity, that is, a purpose or ideal. The question of the purpose of a community is even more important than the question of the structure of a community, because without a purpose, there is no need to have a structure.

What occupies the forefront in most people's minds when considering the current changes in the Church are the conflicts between liberals and conservatives (not to mention radicals and reactionaries). These conflicts often center on issues of authority and institutional change, and therefore it is not strange that people use political terms to define the main positions. The conflicts that have occupied the forefront in Church discussions in recent years have been in many ways an expression of a political controversy in Church life—how the body politic of the Church is to be organized and governed.

But the most important issue facing the Church today is not the political one. It is the question of whether the Church should exist at all. Or, to phrase the question in the terms we have been using, it is the question, why form Christian communities rather than just improve the various natural communities we are in, working together with men who do not accept Christ? Why go to all the trouble to form a special environment? Why have a special grouping at all? Or, to phrase the question a little bit more cuttingly, why should Christianity exist at all? This question enables us to consider a very fundamental area for the vitality of any Christian community and of the Church as a whole—its purpose.

Considering the purpose of the Christian community inevitably leads us to consider questions of spiritual renewal. If we ask what purpose a Christian community has to justify its special existence, we have to deal with Christ and the spiritual life, because this is the area of its special purpose. Approaching the importance of Christ from this point of view, we will be able to see how spiritual renewal has a functional importance, a practical importance, in the life of the Church. Spiritual renewal is not just something that is a "higher value," but does not really enter into the building up of the Church.

Many times people can concede that spiritual renewal is important for Christians today, in fact, of primary importance, and yet still not see how spiritual renewal ties into the way the Church functions. They are faced with a number of problems: structural ones of the kind we have been discussing, problems of declining numbers of priests, financial problems, attendance problems. And they instinctively look for a specific solution to the specific problem (a structural solution to a structural problem, a financial solution to a financial problem, etc.). They can accept the fact that spiritual renewal is important, but they cannot see how it has direct application to the specific problems which are clamoring for attention. And so they naturally try to deal with the pressuring problems first and do not get around to turning their attention to the problem of spiritual renewal.

To understand how spiritual renewal is a practical step in the renewal of the Church, and to see how vital Christian communities can be formed only through centering on Christ, it is necessary to understand:

1) the relationship of the vitality of a community to dedication to its purpose,
2) the importance of the unique purpose of Christianity to the vitality of the Church, and
3) the way in which the renewal of vitality can come.

THE VITALITY OF A COMMUNITY

When a community has vitality, it can do a great deal. For one thing, it is very active. Often we contrast a dead parish with one which is alive. The difference between the two lies in the fact that a parish which is alive has a great deal of activity connected with it. But there are other signs of vitality than activity. Growth is one. A community which is alive, grows. People want to get "where the action is." Another sign of vitality is the effectiveness of activities. When a community or movement or organization is alive, it has an effect on its surroundings and a great impact on the lives of the people who make it up. In one Mexican village, the Catholic Church has many more activities going on than the Communist Party. Yet the Communist Party is running the town and the members of the Communist Party are noted for being more dedicated men. The Communist Party has a much greater vitality in that village.

A community has vitality when it has more resources going into its life and when those resources are well used. A community begins to come alive when its members put a great deal of their time, energy, and money into it. When they do not, it is dead. Many Catholic parishes get only a minimal contribution from most of the parishioners. They come one hour a week, give a dollar or two a week, and hardly expend a thought or a concern on the life of the parish. Their lives are little affected by the fact that they belong to the parish, and the life of the parish is little strengthened by their membership. This is why groups like the Jehovah's Witnesses and the Mormons, even though they are much smaller than the Catholic Church, are much more alive.

When a community is weak or dying, every problem within the community seems insoluble. That is because there is not enough strength, not enough resources in the community to work on the problems. Even if there is enough understanding, problems are still insoluble. But if a community is strong and alive, there does not seem to be any problem which is not a source of greater growth and strength and which cannot be handled. It is just like the human person. If someone is weak and run-down, he cannot handle a disease when he is hit. People with less vitality die more quickly. But if he is strong and healthy, he can come through the disease or injury with much more ease.

Many of the problems facing the Church seem insoluble, not because no solutions can be thought up for problems, but because of the overall lack of vitality and dedication in the Church. What is needed is not primarily better solutions, but a renewal in the life of the Church. The problem of the decline in vocations is a good example. Fewer and fewer people want to become priests. It may be true that better methods of recruiting or more desirable working conditions will be a help in this problem (specific solutions to the specific problem), but an even more fundamental cause is that Catholics are putting less and less of their lives in religion. It does not mean that much to them. The vocations problem is much more a problem of the whole life of the Church and of the dedication of its members than simply a special structural problem that can be worked out by a specific solution.

There are many factors which go into the vitality of

a community. Having a good structure, for instance, is certainly one of these factors. A bad structure can inhibit life, while a good structure can make life possible. A community can have all the resources in the world available to it, and if it cannot use them well, they will not produce much life. An Australian bushman can be much stronger than a senile American. But if the American knows how to use tools better than the bushman, he will be able to be a lot more effective with the strength he has than the bushman will be. In the same way, a good structure to a community will allow the resources that are there to result in a great deal more vitality, while a bad structure may stifle it. Many promising young communities die because the leaders do not have the understanding to know how to deal with the structural readjustments that need to come with growth.

Although there are many factors which go into making a community vital, the most direct source of vitality is purpose and the commitment of the members to that purpose. If a community has a purpose that is clear and compelling, one that seems to be of real importance, and if its members are committed to that purpose and therefore put as many of their resources as possible into fostering that purpose, the community will be a vital community. If the community has no purpose, it will not last, no matter how well-structured it is.

The most stable social groupings we know are held together by a very compelling purpose — survival. Human beings instinctively feel the need to stay alive: to eat, to find shelter, to have protection. They instinctively realize that this happens only in social groupings, and so they have formed tribes, cities, nations. Such social groupings have had a strong hold on those who have been part of them, because they have known that they could not live unless they were a part of such societies.

There have been other foundations for strong communities in our experience. The Communist Party, for instance, has formed a strong worldwide community (a highly organized community). Its vitality and resilience have in great part come from the commitment on the part of its members to the proletarian revolution and to all that is involved in that ideal. The members of the Communist Party have been willing to make great sacrifices of personal interest in order to further the cause. Great causes have mobilized many strong social movements.

A strong, common purpose can result in very effective action. Lack of agreement or consensus can paralyze a group. A political party, for instance, can be much more effective if it has an issue—a strong cause that it can unite around. Dissension over its purposes and directions often is the direct cause of losing many elections. We can see the same thing in the current Church renewal. Many organizations and movements which were strong before Vatican II, all of a sudden lost direction and therefore effectiveness as a result of the lack of consensus produced by the renewal. The Cursillo movement would be a good example. In Mexico the Cursillo movement maintained a clear grasp of a unique purpose and a commitment to it, and it became a strong force in the life of the Church in that country. In the United States after the Vatican Council, every group with an idea made use of the Cursillo movement and as a result, after a strong beginning, the movement lost direction and effectiveness. Recently, there seems to be a reversal of that trend and some renewal in the life of the Cursillo movement in the United States.

There is, of course, a difference between the kind of purpose a community has and the kind an institution or an organization has. An institution or an organization has a particular goal or set of goals. The goal may be to make some product or service available. An automotive company has the goal of selling cars. The telephone company has the goal of making telephone communication available. Or the goal may be to effect a change in society. The American Society for the Prevention of Cruelty to Animals has the goal of changing the attitudes of Americans toward animals. The people who work within institutions or organizations, whether members or employees, are organized to work together to reach the goals of their particular institutions. The more clearly their interaction together is directed toward reaching the goals of the institution, the stronger and more effective the institution will be. A defining characteristic of the social grouping called an institution is that the people in it work together (function in interdependence) either to produce something or effect some kind of change in the world.

A community has a different kind of purpose. Its members do not work together as a community to produce something or to effect a change in society. But in a real community (a group of people with a unity), the members do have a common purpose in the sense of a common ideal. They all live for something. A community fosters something in its common ideal. The members of the community do not work together as a

94

community to achieve a particular goal or set of goals but the fact that the community holds the same ideal means that the members of the community strengthen in each other the commitment to a certain ideal of life, and this ideal forms the lives of each of the members. In other words, the members of the community do not work together (except to build up the community), but they do share a common ideal, and so their lives have a common effect.

The contrast between the peace movement and a peace organization in a particular city makes the difference between the purpose of a community and the purpose of an institution more concrete. The peace movement includes many more people than all the peace organizations put together in this particular city. People belong to the peace movement because of certain convictions. They accept certain values, have certain interests, and are trying to put their lives in the service of peace. They may come to certain lectures, take part in demonstrations, sign petitions. But people can do this and not belong to a peace organization. Peace is an ideal of their lives; it determines many of their actions. But unless they also join a peace organization, they do not work together with others for certain concrete goals like getting a change in a draft law. For a peace organization to exist, the concrete goals must be agreed upon. For the peace movement to exist, each person can have different goals he is working toward, but there must be a common ideal that molds their common life and interaction.

There is, then, a difference between the kind of purpose which a community has and that which an organization or institution has. An organization has a common task toward which work of the members is directed. A community has an ideal of life—it fosters an ideal among its members. It is that ideal that draws them together. But even though the kind of purpose which a community has is different from the kind an organization has, it is no less important for a community to have an ideal than it is for an organization to have a task. In fact, it is more important that the purpose be kept clear and the commitment of the members be kept strong in a community than in an organization, because often a person can be an effectively functioning part of an organization without much of a commitment to the purpose just as long as he is paid, but the life and vitality of the community depend on the free acceptance of the members of the purpose of the community.

In the modern world, the one ideal which everyone can accept is material well-being. Therefore, it is this ideal around which society forms. Nothing is allowed which damages or works against the material well-being of society. A person can convince another person of a falsehood, but he cannot rob him of his material possessions without punishment. But if a special community wants to exist within modern society, it must have an ideal of its own that is important enough to warrant people forming a special community within society. It takes some effort to form a special community in the kind of society we have. Therefore, an ideal is needed which can motivate people to such an effort.

Once we can see the importance of a purpose, an ideal of life, for any community in modern society, then it makes more sense that the Christian community will be vital only if it has a purpose, a reason for existence, and one that its members put a high degree of value on, one that they are committed to. That which is unique about Christianity, its reason for existence, has to be important enough to people that they want to invest time in Christian communities, or Christian communities will have no vitality and eventually cease to exist.

THE UNIQUENESS OF CHRISTIANITY

The question, why should Christianity exist at all, can be reworded: What is unique about Christianity and what is so important about what is unique about Christianity? From this perspective, what Christianity is becomes a vital question facing the Church. It is not merely an academic question.

The question is even more important in view of the present situation of the Church. Christians have to live most, if not all, of their lives in the middle of environments which are not Christian. There is a strong pull from any environment we are in that draws us to become just like the others in that environment. Christians are tempted to become like the people they live with. The question is, then, whether there is anything wrong with that, or whether Christianity has something unique about it, something that makes it worthwhile for men to bother being Christians and belonging to Christian communities.

What then is Christianity? Some common answers are: It is being good (just, charitable, moral), loving others, or having social concern. But a person does not have to be Christian to be good or to love others or to have social concern. Many non-Christians do this. If this is all Christianity is, there is nothing unique about it to distinguish it from simple humanism. The answer does not lie in principles or values, but rather in a person — Jesus Christ. He is what is unique about Christianity. If it is not important to believe in him and follow him, then Christianity is not important. If what he did, his crucifixion, resurrection, and ascension are not important for men to believe in and accept, then Christianity is not important.

An historian once said that when a world religion loses its missionary zeal, that is a sign it is beginning to die. He went on to explain that when the members of a religion no longer feel it important for others to believe in that religion, then they no longer feel it is that important to themselves either. It is no longer considered important enough to justify the special effort to bring it to others. Soon it will no longer be considered important enough to justify a special effort in the person's own life.

The term "important" indicates what we are concerned with. If something is important, it is worth time, effort, and interest. If it is more important than something else, it is worth more time, effort, and interest than something else. It has priority. The fact that toothpaste cuts tooth decay may be as true as that Jesus is the Son of God. But it is not necessarily as important just because it is as true. When tooth brushing occupies as large a place in a Christian's life as Jesus Christ, there is something wrong with that person's Christianity.

If Jesus Christ is what is unique about Christianity, then the purpose of a Christian community is to live for Christ. Therefore, how alive a Christian community will be depends on how important Jesus Christ is to the members of that community. It is rare that a Christian will say straight out that Christ is not important. But many Christians say things that amount to saying that Christ is not important, and that is the source of much of the weakness of Christianity today.

One way of saying that Christ is not important is to define Christianity in a way that does not mention Christ. As was mentioned above, it is very common (if not usual) to hear people define Christianity as "loving others" or something of the sort. Or it is common for them to say that what it is to be a Christian is to be a person who is concerned for others. It is rarer for people to define Christianity in a way that includes the name of Christ. If Christianity can be defined in a way that does not include Christ, then he is not essential. It is a way of playing down the importance of what is unique about Christianity—Christ himself.

A similar way of making Christ less important is to reinterpret certain Christian words. For instance, traditionally the term "faith" meant belief in Christ or acceptance of Christ. "People of God" referred to the members of the Church. It is common today to define faith as, perhaps, "ultimate concern." And it is common today to say that the people of God is "all men." It is true, anyone can define any word the way he wants (there is no law against it, nor can a person be condemned as a heretic on those grounds alone). But when the basic Christian words are defined in a way that does not involve any reference to Christ, then by implication a person is saying that people can have faith (which is important) without having any belief in Christ, or that there is nothing special about belonging to the community of believers in Christ (the Church) since the people of God (which are the people most important to God) are "all men," even if they do not believe in Christ. Reinterpreting concepts is a way of playing down the importance of Christ.

Perhaps the most dangerous form of reinterpreting Christian concepts is reinterpreting the name of Christ himself. The name Christ is applied to "others" or to "all men." "To see Christ in others" or "to serve Christ in my brother" becomes a way of substituting a concern for other men for a concern for the Lord himself. Often people do not seem to know who Christ is. They do not know him as a person in himself—only as a symbol for mankind. Or they see him as a model, as a great teacher, as "the man for others," as the symbol of all that is good. They do not recognize him as the Son of God, the Lord, the Savior, the one to whom they have to come for life.

If Christ is not unique among men, if he is not "the way, the truth and the life" through whom all must go if they are to come to the Father, Christianity is not that important. If all Christ is is a great teacher, an example of a great man, a symbol for mankind or for all that is good in men, Christianity itself is not that important. There is nothing unique about it. What it contains is only what is available in different forms. To reinterpret Christ, or even to teach about Christ in a way that does not bring out his uniqueness as Lord and Savior, is to drain Christianity of all its vitality.

Another way to make Christ less important is to stress certain theological truths rather than others. For instance, the truths that "all men can be saved" and that "we are saved through believing in Christ" are both Catholic teaching. In a real sense they go together. But often people will stress that all men can be saved by living a good life and not that men are saved by Christ. The obvious implication of this kind of stress is that Christ is not as important as living a good life. How the two statements are related is a complicated theological issue, but the implication of stressing that all men can be saved by living a good life is direct and simple: it implies that Christ is not really all that important. There are a number of theological truths which receive a great deal of stress today (like the primacy of conscience rather than the duty to believe in Christ, and the value of all the great world religions as revelations of God rather than Christianity as God's plan for man's salvation). The result is not that error is propagated (these are, after all, truths), but that something other than Christ is being stressed as important.

Another way Christ is made less important is by describing the Christian life mainly as relating to other people rather than relating to Christ. It is a common thing for people to describe Christian living more in terms of loving one's neighbor or following principles of social justice, or fulfilling the duties of one's station in life than in terms of love of Christ, dedication to Christ, prayer, bringing others to know Christ. It is not that such people would say that Christ is not a part of a Christian's life. It is rather that they do not usually describe the Christian life in a way in which he is seen as important.

There are many other examples which illustrate the trend to deemphasize Christ, but one is of particular importance for what we are considering—the tendency to identify more with society as a whole or with some segment of society rather than with the Church. Will Herberg in his book *Protestant, Catholic, Jew* tells about how he gave talks at Catholic schools and would ask the students, "Are you a Catholic American or an American Catholic?" They would almost always answer, "a Catholic American," revealing that they consider themselves Americans first and Catholics second. There is a tendency now for men's primary identification to change from their nation to mankind as a whole (the change has not yet occurred, but it seems in progress). This is happening among Christians, too, and large numbers of them are considering themselves first of all members of the world (of mankind) rather than of their nation. This does not, however, change the situation that Christians do not identify themselves primarily as Christians.

The question of what group a person identifies with first is an indication of what he thinks is the most important. If a person makes his primary identification as a man, he is saying that the things he shares with other men (the desire to survive, perhaps a common human decency) are more important than the things he shares with Christians (Jesus Christ). And, by implication, he is saying that he is not willing to work as hard for Christ (the ideal he holds in common with other Christians) as for the material peace and prosperity of mankind (the ideal he holds in common with all men).

It is true, there is no necessary opposition between the good of mankind and Jesus Christ, quite the contrary. Nor is there any opposition between being a

Christian and being a man or an American. Nor is there any opposition between social concern and Christianity. Again, quite the contrary. But that is not the point. The point is: What will a Christian put his heart into, what will he be dedicated to? If Christianity is to survive and grow in the world, if Christian communities are to be vital and increase, Christians must consider Christ the most important reality in all human life.

Instead, we see something different. We see the Church in a certain sense disintegrating. Groups within the Church are forming community more readily with non-Christians who hold the same values than they do with Christians. It is common to see Catholics feeling closer to some non-Catholics because they are against the war in Vietnam or against Communism than they do to other Catholics because they are Christians. They feel more identification with other members of the anti-Communist crusade than they do with other members of the Body of Christ. They begin to feel less like members of the Church with a special concern and more like members of a party, part of whose life is spent within the hostile institution of the Church or in the inert mass of Christians. Jesus Christ is less of a cohesive force in the Church than different political positions or social values are disintegrating forces.

Another thing we see is people directing their energies away from the specifically Christian. It is common for someone to consider working in the Peace Corps much more readily than working for the missions. It is common for priests and nuns to want to be social workers and psychological counselors (whether they stay in the priesthood and sisterhood or leave) rather

103

than pastors, catechists, and preachers of the gospel. It is common for Christians to consider Christian service exclusively in terms of social action. Evangelism, the service of bringing men to a knowledge of Christ, is not even mentioned.

The primary question which is put to the Church today is, where is your heart, what is most important to you, where is your treasure? The question is, how much value do you put on what is unique to Christianity, Jesus Christ himself? Or, to rephrase, how much importance do you place on forming a community in which life is formed around Christ, in which you will be helped to make Christ the first thing in your life? This is the issue which will decide the future of the Church.

RENEWAL OF CHRISTIAN LIFE

If the vitality of a community depends upon the community having a purpose and the members being committed to that purpose, and if the unique purpose of a Christian community, the purpose that distinguishes it from every other community is its relationship to Christ, then for any real renewal of the Church to take place, the renewal of men's commitment to Christ and knowledge of him is of first priority. Any renewal, in other words, which is not first of all a religious renewal will not renew the life of the Church. This assertion indicates some features that have to be part of any program of overall change in the Church.

First of all, there has to be a renewal in what the New Testament calls "preaching and teaching," or what is today more commonly called "religious education." Central to Christianity is "the service of the word"—communicating to people about Christ and the Christian life. Unless this is done effectively, there cannot be a Christian community. There has, it is true, been a real renewal in religious education in the American Church. No longer do children memorize propositions from Scholastic theology (at least, in most places). But the renewal in religious education has not led to a deeper religious life among Catholics, even though it probably has taken away some of the sources of hostility people had to the old form of Catholicism.

One reason the renewal in religious education has not been as effective as it might have been is a lack of appreciation of the importance of conversion in the Christian life. Education in the Church has frequently been approached as if it were primarily a matter of getting people to accept certain values or principles and sometimes as if it were a matter of acquiring certain information. But a person cannot live as a Christian unless he has made his relationship with Christ the most important thing in his life, that which governs all the rest. In other words, central to education as a Christian are a person's purposes. He must not only accept certain values and acquire some information, he must progressively change his purpose in life so that more and more his concern is to know Christ, to live for him, and to change his life in accordance with what Christ wants. He must make his own that which is the only purpose which can make a Christian community alive— following Christ.

Realizing the importance of conversion has many implications for the life of the Church. First of all, it means a renewal of evangelism in the life of the Church.

"Evangelism" means announcing the good news—telling people about Christ and about his death and resurrection in a way they can realize that they are being invited by God to turn to Christ (convert), change what they are living for (repent), and enter into a relationship with Christ (be baptized). Evangelism is often taken for granted in the Church today. Much religious education is predicated upon the presupposition that the members of the Church have already made a commitment to Christ, even though the kerygmatic school of catechetics has warned that it is fatal to ignore people's basic lack of commitment to Christ.

There has to be a renewal in methods of evangelism. Many religious educators realize the need for evangelization in the Church, but often they do not know how to go about it. They are ready to settle for a process of pre-evangelization that may last for years and never be successful. Yet there are many successful means to drawing people to a commitment to Christ that involves knowing how to shape the message, how to make use of a personal witness, and how to take the concrete steps a person has to take to renew his life. Mormons, Jehovah's Witnesses, Bahais, many of the smaller Protestant sects, dozens of groups in American life know how to preach their own type of life successfully, and much can be learned from them.

There also has to be a renewal in Christian instruction for those who want to live as Christians. Part of this involves a way of bringing new people into the Christian community. The life of the community will suffer if an adequate foundation has not been laid in the lives of those who become part of the community. A sound catechumenate, an initiation process, is needed. There has to, in addition, be solid instruction in an ongoing way for those who are already part of the community. The heart of both the initiation process and the ongoing instruction has to be constantly recalling people to a renewed commitment to the Lord, constantly strengthening the foundations of the Christian life. It is never possible to take the basics for granted.

But even more important than the actual methods of evangelism and instruction has to be the context. In the early Church, and in many Christian groups today, evangelism is the invitation to join the life of a community which holds to the message and is living it. A person is drawn to the community, sees what the message means in daily life, and finds himself attracted by an environment that has more vitality than those he has been in before because it has a strong commitment to a purpose. Even if a Catholic heard a well-preached message in church or in school, he would be unlikely to respond, because his experience (the Christian environment he lives in) has nothing to correspond to the message. It is almost always the case that when evangelism and instruction are done successfully, both in the Church and outside of it, they are done in the context of a community that is alive, and they are done as a means of inviting people into the life of that community or growing in the life of that community. Speaking about Christianity is successful only when it is the clarification of people's experience of the Christian life.

Along with a renewal in evangelism and instruction, therefore, there needs to be a spiritual renewal in the Church. This renewal has to involve a commitment to

Christ, a changing of direction in life, that is true. But it also has to involve a deeper knowledge of God. Christianity is not mainly concerned with an ideal, a value, or a principle, but with a person, a person who can be known. Someone does not become a strong Christian primarily because he sees a way of life which works, but because he comes to know a person, his Creator and Savior. Much of the reason people do not understand the importance of Christ today is that they do not know him. They do not experience his reality, and so they do not experience the difference he can make to a human life.

Many communities are based upon being committed to an ideology or a doctrine or set of values. The peace movement forms around certain values, the Communist Party around an ideology, the Bahai around doctrines. But there is a difference in Christianity which should provide even more vitality than any other community might have. There is a power to Christianity—the power of resurrection, the power of the Holy Spirit. When God is present and at work, there is a life and an effectiveness that cannot be had by mere human means. If men really believe in Christ, they also believe that he is present and at work by his Spirit. Therefore, the spiritual renewal in Christianity must involve knowing how to realize the power in Christianity, knowing how to receive the Spirit and yield to his working, so that through the Holy Spirit in them, the members of the Christian community can do more than they would be able to do as ordinary human beings.

The spiritual life of a Christian community, then, is not merely a luxury. It is the very center of the Christian community. The vitality of the Christian community depends upon the indwelling presence of the Holy Spirit who can give new life to individual Christians and to Christian communities and who can work through individual Christians in charismatic power to build up the Christian community. The very purpose of the Christian life is the knowledge of God through Christ in the Holy Spirit, and if this is missing, a Christian community has no purpose and cannot stay alive.

The importance of the unique purpose of Christianity also has implications for leadership in the Christian community. When it was said that the basic pastoral problem of the Church today is how to build communities which make it possible for a person to live a Christian life, it might have been possible to think that what the Church most needed was sociologists or community organizers. But this is not at all true. What the Church needs most is men of God, men who can and will function as pastors, evangelists, spiritual directors.

The Church needs men of God for a very sociological reason: Communities are not formed primarily by sociologists and community organizers. They are formed by leaders of men who are dedicated to something. Sociologists and community organizers can help a great deal to facilitate the organization of communities, but they cannot substitute for a lack of purpose and direction. They do not provide direction.

This is another way of putting the main point of this chapter. Communities are not formed by focussing attention on forming communities. Nor are they formed by trying to draw dedication to the community itself. They are a by-product, so to speak. They form as a result of dedication to something which is shared. Therefore, the person who is most equipped to form a community is not the person who is an expert in the processes of community but the person who is dedicated to an ideal and who can lead men to it.

The Church needs men of God, then, men who are committed to Christ above all and who are willing to work to bring others to a commitment to him. They must be spiritual men, men who know God, and who can lead others to know him. They must be men who are filled by the Spirit and who are led by the Spirit, men who can work for Christ in the power of the Spirit.

At many points in this section, it was necessary to emphasize that the purpose of Christianity is not loving others or dealing with social problems or community development or anything but Christ. The point is not to play down the importance of these things, but to make apparent the importance of Christ in the process of building Christian community. All these things are involved in Christianity, but if it is important that the beams of a house be placed correctly, it is even more important that the foundation be built well. First things first. The foundation of a Christian community is Jesus Christ. If a Christian community is going to survive, it must have a reason to exist. Its reason to exist is Christ. He is more important to it than anything else. He is the source of its life. Unless there is a spiritual *conversion* in the Church, a turning to Christ and an acceptance of him as more important than anything else, and a spiritual *renewal* in the Church, a deeper knowledge of God and a deeper understanding of how to receive the power of the Spirit, it is fruitless to consider building Christian communities.

5

Pastoral Leadership

The Church today needs leaders who can work with an environmental approach.

For most Americans, communities and environments seem to just happen. They are either there or not. Institutions, organizations, businesses, programs, procedures—these are all developed and planned. But Americans have never seen a community formed. Friendships develop, people interrelate in certain ways, communities emerge. There is nothing it seems that can be done about them, any more than can be done about the weather.

But it is certainly not true that communities cannot be formed purposely. Most people outside modern Western society tend to think that institutions and organizations just happen. For them what we consider ordinary common sense borders on the magical. And just as it is a lack of knowledge that makes some people think that institutions cannot be formed, so it is lack of knowledge that makes us think that communities just happen. There are principles of environmental change and formation. There is a way in which environments function. An environmental dynamic can be learned just the way a production dynamic can be learned. It is possible to learn how to work to form environments and communities.

There is one issue in which all our previous points converge and become acute—the issue of leadership in the Church. None of the above proposals will make any sense unless this issue is resolved. There cannot be more basic Christian communities in the Church unless there are more men who can form them. There cannot be more spiritual renewal in the Church unless there are more men of God. The key to the pastoral difficulties of the Church is, not surprisingly, a supply of men who can do the job.

Not just any men will do. What is needed are men who know how to work effectively. There has certainly been a concern in the Church over how to form men for the most crucial type of leadership, the priesthood. Many options are being proposed and taken. It is being advocated, for example, that priests should be formed in management skills or in psychological counseling or as social workers, or in a variety of other ways. A great number of approaches are being suggested, but if the main pastoral goal is to develop communities in the Church which make it possible for a person to live a Christian life, the principal need is to form leaders for developing Christian communities.

What we are concerned with in this chapter are ways of working to form communities within the Church and with the kind of person who is going to be able to

112

do this work. We are concerned with approaches to Christian leadership, with the dynamics according to which people might work to form Christian communities.

To understand why the Church today needs leaders who can work with an environmental approach it is necessary to see:

1) what an environmental approach is (what kind of approach to working it is)
2) what place activities have in an environmental dynamic
3) what kind of men we must have as leaders to make such a way of working possible.

APPROACHES TO WORKING

People generally are not conscious of the different ways there are to work. If they have a job to do (a community to form or some part of the work of a community to take responsibility for), they will often begin by forming a committee, electing a president, vice-president, secretary and treasurer, and perhaps form a constitution (if they expect the job to take a while) and then think about what is involved in the job and what might be the best way to proceed.

Ways of working, however, raise more important questions than structural ones (even though structural questions are very important). There are a number of ways to work from which a person can choose when something is to be accomplished. There are a variety of processes or dynamics that can be developed which will lead to certain results. Fitting the approach to the job is something which takes a great deal of skill. It is not always good to form an organization or to introduce elective procedure.

The focus in this chapter is on approaches to working, not on structures of leadership. There seem to be three main ways of working common today: the status approach, the functional approach, and the environmental approach. Our purpose here is to clarify what they are and how they relate to the formation of a community.

THE STATUS APPROACH

The Church has in many ways inherited a status approach to the way men work to foster its life. The approach dates back to the time when society was more stable than it is now, and when political life, economic life and social life were dominated by consideration of status. In recent years, there has been a breakdown of status within the Church, but it still exists.

The emphasis in a status approach is on the maintenance of an order that preserves position and stability. Birth, wealth and academic degree have been the most common types of status. One of the primary principles in a status approach, then, is the concern that leadership positions in society (or in a social grouping) be had only by those who have a certain status. For instance, in a political organization that is dominated by considerations of status, a man can become king (that is, chief ruler) not on the basis of any ability as performance, but simply because he has inherited the position (the status of birth). Obedience is due him and the kingdom functions even though he may have no special talents as king.

Something similar is often true of the status that accrues to degrees in an educational organization. In our university system, for instance, one of the chief criteria by which a person becomes a teacher is through the status of having a degree. What he has to do to get that degree may not have any direct relation to what he needs to do as a teacher. To get a degree a person needs to be a good scholar, but degree holders are given positions as teachers and many times no inquiry is made into their ability to communicate to students, nor are they tested on it. The status of the degree will open all kinds of doors, often with no questions asked about a person's competence or about what kind of man he is. (The lack of degree status, on the other hand, will certainly bar even the most competent man from the position of university teacher.)

The same thing has been true of the Catholic priest to a great degree. There have been two status requirements for his selection: a monastic or semimonastic way of life (celibacy being the prime element still maintained) and an academic theological training (four years in the seminary). Both these requirements have some rationale behind them (they are not just senseless vestiges of tradition). Priests do need to be men of God, and an ascetical life should be an aid to that. Priests also need knowledge, and an academic training should be an aid to that. But a person can preserve a life of celibacy and complete a seminary training and still not be an effective priest. The respect accorded the monastic status and the academic status has obscured the fact that they do not qualify someone to be a priest.

In a group which functions according to status, order

is of great importance. A prime consideration is laid upon orderly procedure. Even if a ruler in a status-based society saved the nation, he would not likely be allowed to go unpunished for an infringement of the constitution. A university professor might develop an excellent teaching method for preparing students in a certain area, but if it did not involve giving grades which could be added up for a degree, all his efforts would go unrecognized.

Along with the concern for order goes a concern for ceremony. Normally in status-based societies or groupings, ceremonies have been developed to celebrate the positions of status. Royal courts, parliaments, law courts, universities all have their rituals for conferral of status and celebration of status. As the Church was run more and more according to a status approach, the liturgy became more ceremonious and celebrated more and more the special statuses of priest, bishop, and the other positions in the Church.

A social group which functions by status is also a social group which functions according to tradition. To a great extent the rules by which such a society functions are passed down and accepted as customary. A king who is king because of birth usually finds himself in a position which is rigidly regulated by precedent. What he can do is defined by charter or grant or custom. The teacher in the university system finds his department lines, teaching methods, protocol, etc., to a great extent governed by tradition. It is not much open to change (although, of course, the trend today is away from a status system). The same thing has been true for Catholic leadership. Ten years ago, for a priest not to wear a Roman collar was a serious matter. Although there were good reasons why a priest might want to wear a Roman collar, it is clear from the inflexible nature of the regulation that wearing a Roman collar was enforced because of tradition, not because of those reasons. The Catholic priest of ten years ago functioned in a very traditional role.

Because a group which functions by status also functions according to tradition, it tends to develop a life that is somewhat independent of the people who are part of it. The role is predefined. The person who fits into it does it well or poorly, but it is somewhat irrelevant what he is like. As long as he has that status and the position is vacant, he can fill it, and as long as it is filled, the order of society will continue. The Catholic priest may be a good priest or a poor priest, but as long as he is a priest, he can be the priest for a particular town and the position will be the same no matter who he is or what he is like. Moreover, the people will treat him to a great extent independently of who he is or what he is like. A bad king can still pardon prisoners and a bad priest can still absolve sinners.

It should be noted, however, that although a status approach places a great deal of emphasis on order and tradition, it is not the only approach which uses order and tradition. The functional and environmental approaches may also do so. What defines a status approach is that order is based on considerations of status (birth, wealth, education, etc.) and the status is justified because it is customary. Human beings need order to function together, but the order does not have to be status based and it can be designed by considerations of

117

the need of the group. Order and tradition were important in the early Church, but they were not, for the most part, status based.

A status approach has many advantages. Above all, it is stable. It endures despite individual weaknesses, and to a certain extent it minimizes the problems that can be caused by individual weakness. Moreover, many of the weaknesses of the status approach can be compensated for. For instance, a status approach is particularly vulnerable to having incompetent people in positions of authority, but that tendency can be compensated for by good training and testing of the people before the position is conferred upon them. Where status is a determining influence in human groups, those groups tend to be enduring and they provide a great deal of security for the group members.

The functional approach: The functional approach is best illustrated in the way executives in the modern business corporation work. It is the approach which is above all oriented toward accomplishing something. To an increasing extent, a functional approach is entering the life of the Church today.

The primary difference between the status approach and the functional approach is that the functional approach is much more oriented toward getting results. Everything (in theory) is directed toward getting something done. It seems to be true that considerations of status cannot be eliminated completely but in a functional approach the tendency is in that direction.

According to the functional approach in its pure form, a person's authority should depend on his competence. In an organization run according to a functional approach, there should be no positions which are not functions needed to make the product or accomplish the end intended. There should be no one in any position who cannot perform his function well. Following a functional approach, a person would not be the head of a state if he could not govern well (and this would be judged by the prosperity and harmony in the kingdom), nor would a person be allowed to be a professor if he could not teach well (which would be judged by how much the students learn under him).

A functional approach is in many ways an enemy of tradition. If a tradition is not functional, according to this view, it should not exist. Everything should be weighed from this angle. Wearing a Roman collar should justify itself on utilitarian grounds, as should wearing vestments. Along with this mentality goes an experimental attitude. A person would look around for evidence to tell whether something was functional or not. A man interested in functional effectiveness would want to investigate and see whether a professor's students were actually learning something from him. He would want to check and see what desirable effects come from wearing a Roman collar or what is missing when it is not worn.

A functional approach tends to be rigorous in regard to activities. Where a functional mentality prevails, for instance, ceremony has a hard time maintaining itself. Interpersonal relationships are considered primarily according to how they affect the function involved. A person wanting to use a functional approach first of all wants to define the goal clearly and then wants to order everything so that it furthers the goal.

A functional approach has many advantages. Above all, it is effective. All energies in a system or situation are mobilized to reach the desired end. And it is not true that a functional approach eliminates all consideration of status and interpersonal relationships. Status turns out to have functional value, as do good interpersonal relationships. Even more, many times, a functional concern will stimulate an improvement in interpersonal relationships that would never have come any other way. Often, for instance, a man and wife can be induced to improve their relationship by showing them the bad effects their estrangement is having, whereas trying to motivate them to love each other because love is good or right has no effect at all. Also, a functional approach is flexible. Changes can be made when a reason is shown for them, and change does not have to overcome decades or even centuries of tradition. The functional approach is clearly the most successful in getting a job done.

The environmental approach: An environmental approach is quite different from either a status approach or a functional approach. It is less commonly recognized within the Church today as being a definite approach, but it is nonetheless a real approach, one with advantages of its own.

A functional approach is work-oriented. It is oriented to getting a job done. An environmental approach is interaction-oriented or value-oriented. It is oriented to getting a group of people together who share certain values or concerns. It focusses on the growth of the relationship among people and on how people are being changed for the better. The two approaches are different. Or to put it another way, the work of forming an environment is not the same thing as getting something accomplished. Some business executives are effective at getting production but poor in their ability to draw people together.

There is a definite environmental dynamic that is not the same as a functional dynamic. Management experts sometimes talk about the formal organization and the informal organization. By "informal organization" they mean what we are calling environmental relationships. They mean the voluntary patterns of interaction among the people in the formal organization. They note rightly that the environment in an organization can often have a great effect on the production, even though it is not oriented of its very nature toward production (for example, when workers' attitude toward a company either supports or sabotages the operation).

An environmental approach, then, is one that is concerned above all with the formation of environments or communities. The goal of an environmental approach is to get people to come together, to interact in a personal way, to accept certain values, and not primarily to get something done.

An environmental approach depends on a kind of natural leadership or authority. Certain people have an ability to draw people together, to influence them. Their opinions carry weight, their lives and actions are imitated. From a functional and a status point of view, the teacher is the authority in a classroom, but it is obvious that in some cases a couple of the students are the leaders. They are the ones who indicate what values will be accepted, what attitudes the other students will take, how they will react.

In an environmental approach, the free interaction of the people is much more important than it is in a status approach or a functional approach. It is crucial that the people get to know one another and to begin to form bonds. It is necessary that they freely accept values. In a functional approach, people can be gotten to work either through coercion or pay. In a status approach they will react to the status of the person with authority and to the tradition behind him. But for an environmental dynamic to form, there must be a voluntary acceptance of some values and norms.

During the rest of this section, more will be presented on how the environmental approach works. Enough has been said, however, to indicate that it does have real advantages. It is the approach which most changes people personally. And it provides a way of working when it is impossible to rely on status and tradition (as is more and more the case in the Church today) and when people cannot be motivated through pay or force, but have to be worked with through a voluntary response.

The approach and its place: Isolating the different approaches to working does not imply that one is better than the other. Each one has certain advantages and certain uses. What we need to understand is where each approach is valuable and how we can get it to work effectively when we decide to use it.

What we have been discussing are ways of working,

not different human groups. A business could be run by a status approach (this seems to be one of the main problems in certain sectors of the French economy or in certain American banks) or by an environmental approach (as many times happens in small businesses run by friends or even in sections of corporations). A parish could be run by a status approach (the Church has used this approach with great success at times) or a functional approach (this seems to be one trend in the Church at the moment). In other words, all types of human groups can be run according to one or another of the approaches we have sketched.

Moreover, usually all three ways of working are present to some degree in the same operation. A business today will ordinarily try to structure its activity functionally: to design jobs to efficiently perform certain functions, and to get men with the right kind of skills into the jobs. But it will also usually feel the need to give some of the men in it some kind of status rights for stability (although the trend seems to be away from this) and motivation. And business executives are learning more and more to foster and take advantage of the environments (the informal structure) in the business to try to increase production. Many businesses, in fact, have people whose primary concern is to get a positive environmental dynamic going and they try to make use of an environmental approach.

The same thing is true for forming a community. Status can be an important way of giving stability and solidity to a community (there are few communities that do not eventually feel the need to give certain people a status and authority that do not exactly correspond to their abilities to form community). More-over, a functional approach has its place in a community. Whenever a job needs doing, it is usually worthwhile doing it efficiently. It is true that a well-administered community is not necessarily a good community. But it is also true that if the administration of a community is taken care of efficiently and well, the community life will be that much better if there is also an effective community dynamic in operation.

In addition, the same person can use different approaches on different occasions or in different situations. The pastor of a Catholic parish may be called upon to use all three. In his dealing with the bishop, he may be expected to function primarily in a traditional status-oriented way. He may also be the administrator of a staff, and he may therefore have to operate in that situation using a functional approach. Finally, he may be the priest for the men's group in the parish, and in that situation he may find himself much more effective using an environmental approach, taking advantage of his nattural gifts of leadership, drawing the men together and giving them a positive Christian direction.

Yet, although all three approaches can be used in the same groups or by the same person, it still is true that in some types of human groupings, certain ways of working are more essential than others. In a business, a functional approach is more essential and fundamental. Whatever else a business is, it has to be efficient and its work must be structured effectively in a functional way. In a political body, status and tradition seem to be more valuable than they are in businesses. They further stability and order, and without these even efficient administration cannot accomplish much.

In a community, an environmental approach seems much more essential than a functional approach or a status approach. The main concern has to be the commitment of the members of the community to the purpose of the community and their healthy interaction with one another. The major focus is drawing them together around their ideal of life. If this is not happening, whatever else is happening, they are not succeeding as a community.

Communities, then, are primarily formed by an environmental approach. They begin to come together or develop under the leadership of men who have a commitment to an ideal and an ability to draw men together. These men may not be very good at organization or administration, but they have an ability to give life to a community as a community. In a society that was more traditional and stable, a status approach was an adequate approach for forming a community. People voluntarily reverenced and followed people who had status. But today, this is less and less the case. Because of rapid social change, tradition has little hold, and because of increasing functionalization and democratization, status has less and less influence. An environmental approach seems to be the main one which can form community today.

The point being made is not that organization or structure is useless in forming community. An environmental approach involves a certain kind of organization or structure, but it is not a functional or a status type of organization or structure. It follows natural lines of influence and interaction. Nor is the point that

Christian communities do not have need of, say, management skills or technical skills. These skills have a place where a corresponding function needs performing (and there are functions to be performed in communities). Rather, the point is that the primary skills which are needed are the skills involved in leading men and helping them to relate to one another in a community.

There is today a certain trend within the Church toward professionalization of leadership. Clergy and laymen working for the Church are being viewed more and more as professionals performing professional functions who need professional training. Many of them will, for instance, be trained as counselors and then function according to working patterns similar to those of secular counselors.

Underlying the new professionalism among some clergy is the trend toward the Church becoming more and more of a service organization than a community (sociologically speaking). People are viewing the parish increasingly as a place in which they can get "religious services." As the Church becomes more of a service organization, there is a natural dynamic toward structuring things in a functional way to provide more effective services. When Church workers become more professional, they begin to work more by a functional approach than by an environmental approach.

Professional services are not out of place in a community. But the primary way in which the leadership of a community works cannot be professional (functional) if the community is going to be a community. The Church has to become something more than a service organization if it is going to survive. Unless there is a network of basic Christian communities in the Church, it may become an excellent religious service organization with no one to take the services offered. If communities are going to be formed, they will be formed by men who can work with an environmental approach, and not just as professionals.

ACTIVITIES AND COMMUNITY

Environments and communities can be formed, as has been said. There are principles which go into working effectively environmentally, just as there are principles which go into working effectively functionally. Many of the principles are different, and often a mistake is made by applying the wrong principles in a certain situation (for instance, an organization of a community that is too functional may stifle the free relationships which make community life possible).

One of the most important principles of an environmental approach has been discussed in the previous section on the issue of faith. Environments can be effectively formed around a value. If people are motivated to accept and follow a certain ideal, they will voluntarily feel the need to come together with others who also accept that ideal for support. From this a common life can develop that has great strength. In other words, proclaiming an ideal is one of the most effective ways of forming an environment or a community and in maintaining its strength. Moral power is much more effective in this area than interest or force.

But there is a second principle of great importance in the environmental approach that concerns the activities which are used (meetings, classes, organizations of various kinds). To form a strong environment or community, activities should be designed primarily to further the environmental dynamic. What is meant by "environmental dynamic" is the process of people coming together in a regular ongoing way around an ideal or set of values. Indications of the progress of an environmental dynamic are commitment to the ideal and the cohesiveness of the group. In other words, if the people in a given environment or community are more and more committed to the ideal or values of that community and if they are more and more drawn to one another and have a greater and greater willingness to spend time together and a greater and greater concern for one another, the environment or community is getting stronger.

What an environmental dynamic means for activities can be seen by considering some approaches to the liturgy. Ten years ago, most liturgies in the Catholic Church depended heavily on status and tradition. It was possible to read out of a book everything that would happen in all the Masses around the world, and that book was the way it was because of tradition (tradition explains a service in which the epistle, for instance, was "proclaimed" to the people inaudibly, facing away from them, in a language they could not understand). If a man had the status (ordination), he could fit into any service anywhere and still be adequate. Even if he could not speak the same language as the people or was too old to do much more than make it through the ceremony, he was adequate. Moreover, during the service, he would receive many marks of honor in a ceremonious way (he wore special vestments, people stood to greet him, he partook of Communion separately, etc.). It was very heavily a status-tradition-based happening, and it formed a strong grouping yet without much personal interaction or many personal bonds.

More recently the liturgy has become more functional, in a certain way. If a liturgical event can be viewed as a religious "product" in itself, there has been a functional improvement in the liturgy. People have begun to reflect on the meaning of each part. There has been more explanation. The Mass has been restructured for more effective participation and communication. People have been taught (more often) to read well, to sing well. There has been an emphasis on proficiency in preaching and expressiveness of gesture. From the point of view of the product (a liturgical event), greater proficiency has been developed.

And yet, by and large, even with the increase in liturgical proficiency, most liturgies do not involve an environmental or community dynamic even now. In the liturgy people do not come together and interrelate in a way which forms a community. They do not share a common direction together or form a commitment to one another. It does happen at certain special Masses that communities form, but this is an exception. By and large, we would have to go to certain Protestant churches (usually the smaller sects) or to prayer meetings to see a worship service which is not only satisfying worship but which is also the vehicle for forming a community.

Here is the nub of the distinction between a functional approach and an environmental approach in regard to the liturgy. A functional approach is concerned with getting something accomplished (putting on a worship service, for instance). An environmental approach is concerned with forming a community, developing a real environment of people who are affecting one another. At some worship services, people can be present and very happy with the product without forming any kind of community. At others, the whole service draws people into the community.

The distinction which is being made here is not the distinction between a liturgy which is done mechanically and one which is done with sensitivity and expressiveness. Many liturgies which have all the "communitarian techniques" (the handshake of peace, dialogue sermons, communal singing, spontaneous petitions, etc.) do not foster community at all. The people interact when they are there, but they often have little more tendency to become a community or environment outside the liturgy than the customers at a participative folk sing in a coffeehouse do outside the coffeehouse. It does not lead them to freely form relationships with one another apart from the service. Yet some services (like the one described above in the section on basic Christian communities) do.

A similar point can be made with the example of religious education. Catechism used to depend on status (obedience to the nun) and tradition (memorizing the Baltimore Catechism). Now religious education is often much more professional (better and more effective teaching is done). But it often can fail to reach its goal, because the environmental dynamic is leading the students in the class away from accepting what is given to them, and the religion class is just an educational service — it does not foster an environmental dynamic among the students which might lead them in a new direction.

An environmental approach is a way of working. The primary concern of an environmental approach is to form an environment or a community which centers on certain values. It may make use of a number of activities. It always has some kind of organization or structure (people can do things which are effective at forming community or which are damaging to community formation, and they can learn which things to do and which things not to do), but the organization should always be concerned with the process of forming community.

From this point of view, much of what happens in the Church today is not very effective. There are many activities and many organizations. They do things which are good. But they do not build up a community of people committed to Christ and so they are ineffective in meeting the main pastoral needs of the Church today. It is true, another criterion could be applied to them too. Many of them are not very effective functionally either. Much religious education is not good education, much social action is not effective action. They are usually not evaluated from the point of view of doing effective work. If the Church were primarily an institution which was supposed to provide certain services (educational services, worship services, and social change services) this would be the most serious failure in Church activities and organizations. But if the Church is primarily supposed to be a community of people committed to Christ, there is an even more serious problem—the lack of any community being built up through these activities.

If a person works according to an environmental approach, he would be very cautious about beginning activities or establishing formal organization, especially at first. He would be more inclined to begin with one or two activities which would attract a nucleus of people to a certain value or ideal. As the people began to change and come together, he would introduce activities that would build up the community and whatever organization was needed to meet the experienced needs. Above all, he would be careful not to drain off energy into activities and organization that was needed to form the community. In other words, he would keep a careful eye on the process of community formation (the environmental dynamic), and he would evaluate all activities and organization from the point of view of whether they were deepening the commitment of the members of the community to the ideal and deepening their bond with one another. Eventually, when the community was strong enough, out of the community would come many services which would be much more effective because they would be guided by an ideal and maintained by people with a strong commitment.

To translate what has been said into more Christian terms, a person working pastorally according to an environmental approach would be very wary of starting organizations and activities. Nor would he be inclined to spend a great deal of time in shoring up most of the present parish and diocesan organizations and activities. Many of them lack any sense of community, are ineffective, and are dying. He would be much more inclined to begin by drawing together a nucleus of people

who would be strongly committed to Christ and who
would begin to share together their life in Christ. Then
as the community developed, he would gradually begin
to add activities and organization, but only so long as
those things furthered the commitment to Christ and to
the community. Only later on might he be inclined to
consider significant educational or action programs—
when there were people ready to work on them and when
they would not drain the strength of the community
away from the life of the community and from commitment to Christ. Moreover, when he would form any
activities, a primary concern would be to see that the
people involved in those activities would grow in their
commitment to Christ and to each other as a result of
taking part in them.

What we have said in this section about the place of
activities in an environmental approach is not the same
point that was made in the first chapter on the holistic
approach. It is possible to have a holistic approach to
activities and still use a functional rather than an environmental approach. A pastor of a parish could view himself as the chief manager of a religious institution that
provides effective religious services. If he were a good
manager, he would be concerned with the goals of the
institution and the successful operation of the units of
the institution taken as a whole. But he would not be
trying to build a community. He would not view himself as a pastor concerned to form the members of his
parish into a basic Christian community. He would
probably tend to approach services (like the liturgy) as
ends in themselves, that which his service institution is
trying to provide for the people, and the criterion he

would use to evaluate them would be their success as worship events. He would be less inclined to view services as instruments to form community or to evaluate them according to the criterion of whether they bring people together in Christ or not. He would, in other words, be using a holistic approach, but he would not be using an environmental approach. He would be combining a functional approach to working with his holistic approach.

To summarize this section, one of the most important principles of an environmental approach is that all activities in a community be viewed from the point of view of whether they are furthering an environmental dynamic, a coming together of the people in a common dedication to the Lord. There are certainly other ways of viewing them, and those other ways can be valuable. A community worship service does not have to be sloppy. It can be a good service considered in itself as well as a means of forming community. But the primary way of viewing activities in a community is whether or not they strengthen the life of the community.

FINDING LEADERS FOR COMMUNITIES

If the Church can be built up effectively only by an environmental approach to pastoral work, then the primary need is to find men who can use an environmental approach, that is, men who can build communities. There has to be a way of finding the right kind of men, forming them to do the work, and fitting them into the right place in the right way.

A leader in a Christian community has to do three things. First of all, he has to be able to present the ideal on which the community is based in such a way that people will understand it, accept it, and grow in commitment to it. Secondly, he has to be able to draw people together and to get them to relate to one another in a positive way. Finally, he has to be able to provide whatever organization is needed to see that everything which is needed for the people to live according to this ideal (or in the service of this ideal) is provided.

Or to state the point more explicitly, a Christian leader has to be able to draw people to Christ and to help them to grow in their relationship with Christ; he has to be able to help people come together to form community based on Christ; he has to be able to organize the community in such a way that people get all the help they need to be good Christians—in that order of importance. In order to get a good community dynamic developing, a leader has to do those three things.

If a man is working to form community with an environmental approach, he will tend to approach the way in which he leads people somewhat differently than he would if he were working with a status approach or with a functional approach. If he were working according to a status approach, he would be much more likely to give orders or to operate by authority. If he is working according to a functional approach, his concern would be more with establishing procedures, defining responsibilities, teaching skills, keeping records, etc. But if he is working according to an environmental approach, he would mainly try to lead people to Christ, to help them to understand how to live the Christian life, to encourage them to make a deeper commitment to Christ, and to encourage them to take more of a responsibility for the common life. He would, to a great extent, be using personal influence.

In an environment or a community, the functions a person performs for the common life or the position he holds in the community structure is not necessarily a good indication of his leadership. The leadership of an environment is not necessarily provided by the people who run it organizationally or who preside over it. In a classroom the teacher is the head organizationally, but some of the students may be the real leaders of the environment. In a political group, the president may not be as influential as certain prominent members who might be, for instance, the real spokesmen for the group. In a Christian community, many people might be more influential in drawing people to Christ and in holding the community together than the official head.

There is, in other words, a difference between position or job and leadership. Having a position or job in a community does not guarantee the kind of leadership a person exercises. There is a need to look at more than job or position when the question of the formation of a community is raised. The more important question is who are the people whom the others follow. If the structure of a community does not include the real leaders, it will not be very effective in the long run.

In a community there is one basis for leadership which is most important. In a status situation, leadership can be established through having a certain kind of status (perhaps birth or wealth or scholarship) that may not have a direct relationship to the job to be done. In a task-oriented situation, the leadership is established in a more functional way—the ability to perform a function or do a job well, i.e., competence. But in a community, effective leadership is established in a different way. That person is a leader in the community who has the ability to influence men, to draw them to accept certain values and approaches, to motivate them to form a community. In a certain sense, this kind of leadership is functional (in a way that status leadership is not) but it is functional in a different way from functional leadership in a task-oriented situation. The chief criterion of effectiveness is not ability to get work done but the ability to get men to respond in a voluntary way.

The key to finding the man who can be an effective leader in a community is to see what man carries weight with others, what man changes people's opinions and decisions, what man others tend to identify with. Leadership of this sort depends on having certain gifts, gifts which could be natural or charismatic. Some people seem to be born leaders of men. Others, by holiness of life or special workings of God in them, have a spiritual authority. Often these two factors are combined or work in some kind of combination. Sometimes, considerations of status or competence in a job are important factors in natural leadership. In a society where birth or an academic degree carries weight, these can be real considerations (although a man who has status but no leadership gifts will rarely be a good leader). Sometimes skills, especially organizational skills or speaking skills, are real considerations. But the chief criterion should be the ability to foster the development of a community.

In the attempt to find leaders for communities, the selection process is more difficult than it is in a situation in which it is possible to work according to a status approach or a functional approach. In a status approach, a person can be picked out fairly directly (if he has a certain parentage, or if he has a degree, or if he has spent time in a certain situation). In a functional approach, a person can be picked by seeing how well he functions in certain jobs. He can be given jobs to do which will be an indication of how well he could do jobs which involve a similar function. But in an environmental approach, he has to emerge as a leader. He can be picked well only by observing what kind of effect he has on others and how they accept him as a leader.

A good term for the type of leadership that is natural to a community is "elder." An elder has a position. He is one of the recognized heads, and he has an openly accepted responsibility for the order of community life. But he is chosen because he really is one of the elders, and not only in name. He is chosen because he has a natural position of respect and leadership in that community. His opinions and decisions "count" more than most people's anyway. That would be true even if he did not have the position. In a properly functioning community, the position reflects the reality.

Although the elder represents a natural type of leadership, in a Christian community elders are not picked because of natural qualities alone. Because the Christian community is spiritual, its leadership is spiritual. The elder in the Christian community has a "spiritually natural" place within the Christian community. Some of that place comes from natural qualities, but more of it has to come from maturity and wisdom in the Christian life.

The elder was traditionally the leader of the Christian community. Early Christian communities, like Jewish communities and many pagan communities, had elders as heads. In the Catholic Church, the priest is supposed to be an elder. The theological statement of his position is that he is elder or presbyter. The meaning of his office has been somewhat out of focus in recent times. Emphasis has been placed on the sacramental part of his office as a special "minister" and on his status as part of a "clerical" body, and recently on his professional training (where that is present).

If the Church is going to be able to return to a community life, the position of elder has to be recaptured. Leaders are needed who can work with an environmental approach, and they have to be the kind of people who have a "spiritually natural" authority. It is only when we have the kind of leadership which is appropriate to community life that we can have successful communities.

At this point, it is important for the sake of clarity to qualify what has been said. So far, we have been talking about the need for the right kind of leaders of communities and how they have to be selected by observing the effect they have on others and how they emerge as leaders. If a community is going to form, there have to be such leaders to provide the backbone for the community. But in a community which is not too tightly structured, there is room for a great many types of people working to form the community. A place can be found for a person whose abilities are primarily administrative or for a person whose abilities are primarily those of a teacher. In other words, there can be a team of people in the community who are contributing to the formation of the community so long as there are one or two or more who can provide the core leadership which can create a community dynamic. Or to state it another way, elders are not the only ones who should be providing leadership for a community.

A second clarification is an elaboration of something which was said before: Using an environmental approach does not mean that officially recognized positions are out of place. As a matter of fact, it is usually important early in the development of a community for some people to be given recognized positions for the stability of the life of the community. This is where ordination should come in. Ordination is the conferral of a special position, a special authority, on someone for the good order of the community. The approach we have been sketching does not eliminate the need for ordination, neither sociologically nor sacramentally. But it does give some indications about when ordination should be conferred and on whom.

If the Church is to work toward new structures of communal life and new forms of pastoral leadership, there are going to have to be some major changes in the present form of choosing leaders. This is true of both lay and clerical leaders. First we can consider some of the implications for clerical leaders of what we have said.

To begin with, there is need for a new method of selection for ordination. At the moment, a person volunteers to be a candidate for ordination. If he meets the basic mental, physical, and psychological standards, he is admitted to the seminary. If he completes the seminary program in a satisfactory way, he is ordained and then assigned a place to work. But the seminary approach is inadequate as a process of selection. It is inadequate primarily because it does not provide any way for the candidates to prove their capability for leadership in community. Throwing in a year or two of special pastoral work does not do the job either. There has to be a way of seeing which men can as a matter of fact lead other men closer to Christ and form Christian communities. This can be done only as a person is actually working in a functioning community, not in prestructured environments (like seminaries), nor in special projects (like most pastoral training programs).

Watching for leaders as they emerge does not mean making the mistake of picking the people who are already in Church organizations, because they are usually there because they volunteered and are frequently ineffective in forming Christian communities. Nor does it mean electing people, because there is not enough community in the Church today where an election would be a good indication of how the community accepts a person as a leader (since most of the electors would not know him). It means observing where real Christian communities are being formed effectively and picking the people who are responsible for that process. Ordination in the Church will be most effective when those who are ordained are the natural leaders of the Christian people.

The seminary approach is not only inadequate as a way of selecting priests, it is also inadequate as a process of formation. The primary criterion of success in seminary training is academic. It is the ability to pass courses. It therefore fits a person primarily for a position as a theology student or scholar. Often an uneducated Protestant inner-city minister is more effective as a former of Christian community than a seminary-trained priest in an inner-city parish, because the minister knows how to lead his people. The principal formation a person needs for leadership in a Christian community is a deeper relationship with Christ and the skills of leading people to accept him and of forming communities (neither of which is best acquired by courses). This is not to say that instructional training is of no value. Anyone who is actually engaged in forming Christian communities will feel a need for knowledge about Christianity and about the situations he is encountering. But it is to say that the *focus* of seminary training is off if the seminary is the *main* way of forming priests.

A further implication of what has been said is that we need a great many more leaders in the Church than we have today. If we are going to move toward bringing people to basic Christian communities, more pastors are needed. At the moment, less and less people are being ordained. There are three possible approaches to this situation: letting a greater and greater leadership vacuum develop in the Church, letting an unordained leadership grow up until the leadership in the Church functions with little relationship to the sacramental system, or making the present approach to leadership in the Church more flexible. Only the last-mentioned seems to make good sense.

Actually, many of the suggestions made above are designed to handle the leadership scarcity in the Church. The main reason fewer and fewer people are interested in the priesthood and other positions of leadership in the

Church is that Christianity and the Christian community do not mean as much to them as secular ideals. The environmental pressures are leading them away from wanting to put much of their time into the life of the Church. But vital Christian communities provide a continuing supply of leadership. One reason, therefore, for moving in this direction is that even though it would take more leadership to accomplish, it will provide more leadership in the long run. In fact, it is the only approach which will, because people will not make that kind of commitment of their lives if they are not part of some Christian community or a strong Christian environment.

One implication of what has been said so far might seem to be that those who have been selected and formed in the present system are inadequate for the pastoral work of the Church today. This is not, however, a necessary implication. First of all, even though the system has not been designed to provide pastoral leadership of the kind we have been considering, that does not mean that many of the people who have been ordained are not the right kind of people for the job. Some are not, but many are. Secondly, as was pointed out above, there is need for many kinds of contributions for the formation of the Church. The kind of community formation leadership working through the environmental approach we have been considering is not the only kind of work that needs doing to make the Church grow and develop. Finally, the present priests have been trained to work in the present approach to maintaining the life of the Church. A whole new approach is not something in the immediate future.

Although the ordained priesthood is the most crucial element in the leadership of the Church today, lay leadership is important too. In our present situation, most leadership positions have to be filled by laymen or leadership needs will not be met. But even ideally, ordained elders are not the only form of leadership a good community needs. For a community to function well, many people who are not ordained have to perform roles of leadership or take positions of leadership.

The present approach to getting lay leadership in the Church is inadequate for many of the reasons the approach to clerical leadership is inadequate. Normally, the way it is done is to set up organizations and activities and ask laymen to volunteer. Those who do then sometimes receive some training. Occasionally elective procedures are used, but the elective procedures usually amount to a choice between volunteers. Those who are willing to take the jobs get them. Too often the people who are in positions of lay leadership in the Church would not be naturally accorded leadership.

The same approach to choosing clerical leaders should be adopted for choosing lay leaders. In a community, certain leadership patterns gradually emerge. Different members of the community become visible as people with special gifts for certain kinds of leadership. These would be the ones who would be asked to fulfill the appropriate functions in the life of the community.

Basic Christian communities, new communal structures, and new patterns of leadership go together. As one develops, the others have to develop. Much of what has been said about forming communities would be utopian if there were not leaders who could do the job.

Or the approach to leadership selection sketched above would be impossible if there were not real Christian communities in which they could develop. The two grow together. This type of leadership actually develops quickly in an environment of free interaction if there is good direction. Such a community provides leaders who are committed and who know instinctively how to form community. It is not a question of which comes first, the chicken or the egg, but of a little capital wisely used which makes more. A new approach to community has to be implemented by the right people, but they will begin a process which will lead to more community and more leaders.

6

Movements in the Church

Constructive social change in the Church today should be fostered through the intelligent use of movements. Liturgical movement, Christian Family Movement, Cursillo movement, civil rights movement, ecumenical movement, peace movement, Pentecostal movement, et cetera, et cetera—the Church is filled with movements, some growing, some declining, some new, some old. There is a great deal of activity in the Church today, many people trying to further many causes and make many changes. The great variety of activity (and of movements) is a sign of life. The various efforts being made to change the Church are one indication that the Church is not dead.

But changes and movements are not an unmixed blessing. They may be a source of new life and of improvements in the Church, but they are also a source of problems and have been damaging to the life of the Church. If the adherents of each of the movements in the Church were asked to draw up a list of the benefits that the movement brought and the critics were asked to draw up a list of the disadvantages they brought, each group could come up with a list, and each could make a good case for his list. Movements may be good, but they are not automatically good, and their effects are rarely wholly good.

It is a perennial temptation for men to choose stability rather than change. Stability is easier. In stable circumstances, a man knows what he will have to cope with. If, for instance, food always costs the same, it would be easier for people to manage money. Every week they could make the same amount of money and handle it the same way, and they would be able to eat. There are, of course, some people who prefer change to stability, or, more precisely, who prefer more change than others do. But today, whether we prefer change or stability is an academic issue. Society is undergoing social change at an ever more rapid rate. It is no longer possible to try to have a stable society in the sense in which even our parents knew it. In order to survive, we need to come to terms with change.

Many families today have people who came over from "the old country" when they were young. They did not learn English very well because they did not have to. They came to neighborhoods in which everyone knew their language. But times have changed. There are few of those old neighborhoods left. And the older people who never learned English are out of communication with most of those around them. They are completely dependent on other people's good pleasure in order even to survive. A Church which did keep pace with the changes in society might find itself in an even worse situation.

147

The subject of the place of movements in the Church is a slightly different one from what we have been considering. The need to form special Christian communities, the basic structure of whatever communities are formed, the importance of spiritual renewal for the vitality of those communities and the type of leadership which is needed for those communities form a tightly knit whole. It would be very difficult to treat one of those subjects without treating the others.

But the question of social change is so pressing for the life of the Church today that the question of movements needs some consideration. The kind of renewal and restructuring we have been considering will not be possible without the help of movements. Other instruments are going to be needed besides movements (institutional changes, development of methods, etc.), but some sort of movement(s) will be necessary to move the Church in the direction we have been discussing.

Moreover, the use of movements fits in closely with the approach we have been considering. So far in this book, we have developed the position that what is needed for an effective renewal of the Church is more than institutional changes. The primary need is to learn to make use of environmental forces and to create environments in the Church. Using movements is one way of using environmental forces, and the place of movements in the life of the Church can be most easily understood in the context of the principles we have been enunciating.

We need a policy toward movements. By "policy" is not meant a new set of canons, nor a set of diocesan regulations. Rather, what is meant is more general wisdom and understanding (which may or may not be embodied in canons or regulations). Movements can be one of the most valuable forces in the life of the Church if they are understood and guided wisely. In order to see how constructive social change in the life of the Church today can be fostered through the intelligent use of movements, we have to grasp the following points:

1) that movements are forces (trends) of social change,

2) that movements can be made use of to change the life of the Church in a beneficial way, and

3) that movements must be integrated into the life of the Church so that the social change they lead to is constructive.

MOVEMENTS AS SOCIAL CHANGE

There are, for our purposes, three kinds of change in human society: organic processes, growth, and social change. Organic processes are the kind of changes which any human group (or organism of any sort) needs to go through just to stay the same. One example of organic processes can be found in the human body. Our bodies are constantly changing: blood is moving, nerves are sending signals, glands are secreting hormones. In fact, every seven years, we are told, our body has been completely renewed. If these changes did not occur, we could not stay the same. If our blood, for instance, stopped changing its place in the body, we would be dead in a matter of minutes.

The same sort of changes are found in human groupings. In a corporation personnel is replaced, messages travel, materials are moved. These changes happen constantly. If they did not, the corporation could not stay the same. It would soon come to an end. Such changes can be called organic processes. Organic processes are the constant changes which allow any social grouping to stay the same, to maintain its size and pattern.

A second kind of change is growth (or decline). This type of change is simply a change in size, which sometimes leads to a change in structure. A basic Christian community, for instance, might grow steadily over a period of years. Then it might split, and two communities might be formed. Or they could decline, or remain stable in size. Growth does not necessarily imply a change in the patterning of life in a social grouping.

The third kind of change is social change. Social change is a change in the structures and patterns of life of a social grouping. Social change could affect part of a grouping or the whole grouping. It could be superficial or fundamental. It could be constructive or destructive (or neutral). In the Church, the institution of the diaconate, a large number of people accepting birth control, the decline of novenas, the formation of floating parishes, the starting of parish councils, all are instances of social change. Each involves a transformation of the life patterns of the Church.

Often social change is necessary for the health of a social grouping. Sometimes social change is necessary in order to give greater vitality to a social group which is not functioning as well as it should. Liturgical renewal could be looked at from this point of view. One of the main reasons why many people promoted liturgical renewal throughout the Church was to provide greater vitality for the life of the Christian people.

Sometimes social change is necessary to make the life of the social grouping more adequate to the changing situation in which it has to live. The Christian Family Movement was begun because there was a need to make Christian couples aware of the implications for their lives of technological society. Couples were organized to take part in what was called the social apostolate.

Usually, any social change will involve both the attempt to revitalize a social grouping and the attempt to adapt it more effectively to the living situation. Neither can be done very successfully without also doing the other. The Vatican Council was called primarily to renew the Catholic Church and to make it more effective in its mission, but one of the major concerns throughout the Council was the *aggiornamento,* the updating of the Church. Each fed the other and needed the other.

In a rapidly changing world, social change has to be considered a regular part of the life of any social group that wishes to survive. Modern business corporations in the last couple of decades have developed offices of research and development (planning) in order to keep their organizations abreast of the changing technological and economic situation in which the business has to function. They are trying to institutionalize social change. Every group has to find ways of doing this, even if it does not have to set up special departments to do it. The group which is closed to social change in today's world is unlikely to survive, not to mention make headway.

Social change can come in a variety of ways. Perhaps the most common way is through diffusion of information and values. Most changes in consumer patterns, for instance, come through diffusion of information and values by word of mouth and advertising. Institutional sponsorship is another source of social change. The American government can decide that new ecological practices and values are necessary, and by some legislation and administrative action can change social patterns throughout the country. The influence of models and successful programs (usually spread by diffusion of information) is another source. A group of hippies begin a commune and their influence leads to other communes. Finally, social change can come through movements.

Movements are often one of the most successful responses to the need for social change. A movement is a special environment which develops because of people's advocacy of some kind of social change. It is a type of voluntary interaction among people which exists because of those people's commitment to a change in the way the life of society or some part of society is patterned. In other words, there are two things which define a movement—it is an environment, and it is formed because of the acceptance of some ideal of change.

A good example of a movement is the liturgical movement. The liturgical movement began as different people developed a sense that something important was missing in the life of the Church, namely, an appreciation of public worship. This new awareness began with a very small group of people. As is the case with most new patterns of social life, the new awareness spread from person to person. A bond was created among these people because of the new interest. They would have regular contact, informal at first, about their new interest. As the liturgical movement spread and more and more people began to develop the interest, various organs of interaction emerged: magazines, books, meetings, study sessions, eventually even courses, permanent commissions, and conferences. The result was a larger and larger group of people who began to appreciate the values of the liturgical movement until the point where it was accepted by the Church as a whole and, for all practical purposes, the liturgical movement ceased to be a specific movement within Catholicism.

A movement is not the same as an organization. In an organization (an institution) all the members work together in functional interdependence to produce something or to make some kind of change. In a movement, the people do not work together in functional interdependence. Rather, they are a group of people who are committed to fostering a certain kind of change.

Sometimes it may be difficult to distinguish between an organization and a movement, because some voluntary organizations seem very similar to movements. The Legion of Mary, for instance, has many of the characteristics of a movement. The members belong to the Legion because they hold certain ideals and want to see certain changes. They often have a commitment to the group of people they are with, a commitment that goes beyond their actually working together in the Legion. It has, in other words, a certain "spirit." But the Legion is not, strictly speaking, a movement, because it primarily exists as a group of people who work together to get some job done.

It can also be difficult to distinguish between organizations and movements because some movements are organized. The CFM and the Cursillo movement, for example, are relatively highly organized movements. Each has one organization which fosters the whole movement (not, of course, in anything like the highly organized way in which a business corporation or a political party would function). Moreover, there are organizations which further movements and so could be considered a part of the movement. *The Liturgical Bulletin* or the National Liturgical Conference were organizations which furthered the liturgical movement. But even in an organized movement like the CFM or the Cursillo movement all the members of the movement do not work together in functional interdependence to get a job done (the CFM is perhaps a borderline case, but in theory and usually in practice it is a movement, not an apostolic organization).

It is more difficult to distinguish movements from communities than to distinguish movements from organizations. Both movements and communities are united (drawn together) by some common ideal or value. But the distinction lies in the concern for social change. Something can be termed a movement when it is primarily united in a desire to make a change in the present situation. But something is termed a community when it is primarily concerned about maintaining an ongoing life, no matter what the present situation.

One of the characteristics of movements is that they tend to become communities or to dissipate as movements and leave institutions to carry on the program. The Franciscan movement, for instance, was a movement of spiritual renewal in the medieval Church. At an early date it was organized and eventually became more a community which fostered a special spirit among those who joined than a movement for spiritual renewal. Methodism was a movement of spiritual renewal within the Church of England. After a while, it separated from the Church of England and became a church of its own, a community. Or the liturgical movement was a movement while it was a recognizable group of people drawn together by their desire for reform in the liturgy (or by their acceptance of the importance of the public worship of the Church). During the Vatican Council, the goals of the liturgical movement were accepted by the Church as a whole, and the movement dissipated, leaving National Liturgical Week, liturgical institutes, *Worship* magazine, etc. The more the concerns of the liturgical movement are accepted by other groups and institutions, the more it disappears as a unique movement.

Movements differ in the kinds of change they seek to further. Some want to renew certain dimensions of the life of the Church. The liturgical movement, for instance, formed out of a concern to strengthen the public worship of the Church. The charismatic renewal formed out of a concern to deepen the experience of the presence and working of the Holy Spirit in the life of the Church.

Some movements, however, are formed to change certain values in the lives of Christians. The peace movement began in a desire to eliminate the commitment of Christians to wars (or at least to *all* the wars sponsored by their own governments). The Christian Family Movement was begun to spread certain values of social action and family life. Moreover, some movements are formed to get Christians to do certain things. The Cursillo movement was founded (originally) to get Christians to work apostolically in the situations they lived in, that is, to work apostolically in an unorganized way.

Movements also differ in the kinds of structures and activities connected with them. The liturgical movement, for instance, fostered a set of practices which could be made part of a Mass (dialogue, singing, the altar facing the people, the use of English, etc.). Wherever a number of these practices were accepted, there was a "liturgical" Mass. The Christian Family Movement has involved a type of study-action group meeting for formation and occasional weekend study sessions. In fact, the movement hardly existed apart from participating in those meetings. Something similar is true of the Cursillo movement which (where it has followed its original design) was structured by the Cursillo weekend, the ultreya, and the group reunion. The charismatic renewal is a combination of a set of practices (praying with people to be baptized in the Spirit, praying with them for healing, speaking in tongues and prophecy, spontaneous worship, etc.), and an informally structured type of meeting (the prayer meeting and the Day of Renewal).

Not all movements in the Church are Catholic movements. Some movements are movements in society as a whole which have many adherents in the Church. The peace movement is primarily a society-wide movement. There are many Christian peace groups, but the movement as a whole has been a secular movement (with religious roots) which has made significant changes in the Catholic Church. The human relations movement (the movement which centers around T-groups and "sensitivity training") is a secular movement which is beginning to have a significant impact in the Catholic Church and to form a special environment. Some movements are ecumenical movements, Christian movements that affect Christians in all kinds of Churches. The charismatic renewal would be an example of this, as would the liturgical movement to a less significant degree.

Movements are not the only kind of social change, but movements are one of the most effective sources of social change. In considering how to renew the Church, it would be a mistake (one sometimes made) to neglect the role of movements.

MAKING USE OF MOVEMENTS

A movement, as was said in the previous section, is a special environment which develops because people advocate some kind of social change. In other words, all movements involve an *environment* (a grouping, an interrelationship, a drawing together of people) and a *value,* the value which people want to see realized. In addition, as has been pointed out above, movements also bring with them structures and practices which have been developed to foster the movement. All three aspects of a movement (its dedication to a value, the environment it creates, and the structures and practices connected with it) are sources of contributions a movement can make.

The most obvious use of movements, therefore, is to further the values in the Church which they were formed to further. Sometimes, movements form to revitalize the life of the Church, or some aspect of the life of the Church. One of the chief effects of the liturgical movement, the CFM, the Cursillo, and the charismatic renewal has been simply to bring the people touched by them to a deeper dedication to Christ and the Church. Since people's attitudes, values, beliefs, and behavior patterns are affected by their environments, when they are touched by or drawn into a movement which is dedicated to renewing the life of the Church, they become more dedicated Christians, and their increased dedication contributes to revitalizing the Church.

Sometimes the impact of movements is toward reorienting the life of the Church, toward making the kind of adjustments which the Church needs in order to be more effective in the modern world. For instance, the Cursillo movement was designed to foster (among other things) a certain kind of evangelism (a natural, unorganized, "environmental" evangelism) in the Church. Since the Church is going to need evangelism to the extent that it cannot depend upon men being Christians because of environmental support, the Cursillo movement is working toward an adjustment which the Church needs and the Vatican Council recommends (DLA 6, 13). The same thing is true of the charismatic renewal. The charismatic renewal fosters (among other things) a desire for worship. The more the developments of modern society make people less and less satisfied with performing formal worship out of duty, the more the Church needs movements which lead people to a spontaneous, freely chosen worship.

In short, the main use of movements is to achieve the social changes which the movements are developed to further. Movements are effective in making these changes, because one of the best ways new values are accepted is through people who are committed to those values by their own choice and who want others to accept them.

There are, in addition, other benefits which movements have brought which might be considered by-products of the movements, but which for pastoral purposes are very important. One of the prime by-products of movements is that they do create new groupings of people (they are, after all, "environments," and having a movement is one way of getting an environment formed —drawing people together out of dedication to a cause). When a new grouping of people is needed, a movement can be a very effective instrument to get it started.

We can consider, for instance, the example of a typical Catholic parish with a pastor who wants to renew the parish. One of the chief obstacles he runs into is parishioners who do not want to change. In many parishes around the country, movements have been used to great effect in dealing with this problem. Sometimes the change in parishioners' attitudes has "just happened" as movements like the CFM and the Cursillo have spread. In other cases, skillful pastors have spotted the potential of these movements and introduced them into their parishes for the purpose of finding groups of laymen they could work with to revitalize the parish.

A good example is a parish in a Midwestern town. The pastor became alive to the need for Church renewal through the Vatican Council. But he faced a parish with the traditional activities made up of people with traditional attitudes. Moreover, few of the laymen would have been considered dedicated Christians (although, of course, there were many "loyal" Catholics). By using the Cursillo movement, he created a new grouping in the parish who related to one another, to the parish, and to Christianity in a new way. Moreover, because of the religious change they had gone through as a result of the Cursillo, they were open to other kinds of changes. They were a nucleus which formed the basis for a thoroughgoing renewal in the parish. Parishes like this are the exception rather than the rule, because pastors who understand the potential of movements are the exception rather than the rule, but there are enough parishes like this to show that movements can be very valuable in creating new groupings of people in the Church.

This use of movements to create new groupings indicates the value of movements for dealing with one of the problems we considered before: the problem of forming basic Christian communities. When the result of a movement is to create a nucleus of people who are committed to one another and to Christianity in a new way, this group of people can become the source for the formation of a basic Christian community. It can form around them and, as it forms, their previous specialized interest can become the beginning of a more complete understanding of what a Christian community should be like (members of movements tend to see only their "cause" at first but after the initial enthusiasm they begin to see other needs as well).

A second by-product of movements is that they do bring innovations which can be of use in the life of the Church. Sometimes these innovations are practices which can be learned from the movements. For instance, the prayer of the faithful was learned from the liturgical movement and is now a common practice in the whole Church. A certain kind of group dynamics was learned from the Cursillo movement and is now used broadly throughout the Church outside the Cursillo movement. In other words, movements are sources of creativity.

Sometimes these innovations are new structures. For instance, the Franciscan movement in the 12th century very early was formed into the Franciscan orders which proved to have an enduring value in the life of the Church. The Cursillo movement has developed the ultreya and the group reunion which conceivably could become standard structures in the Church, fostering a certain kind of evangelism among lay leaders. In other words, movements can develop some of the needed new structures to enable the life of the Church to thrive.

There are, in short, a number of uses which movements can have in the life of the Church. They can be used to revitalize the Church or an aspect of the life of the Church, they can be used to adapt the Church better to the situation it finds itself in, they can be used to create new environments and groupings where these are needed, and they can be a valuable source of innovations in the life of the Church. But, as was said before, there are other means of social change besides movements. There is institutional sponsorship (as illustrated by the Vatican Council and the changes it produced), there are organizations and organized efforts (like the Legion of Mary), and there is diffusion of values and information (changes in the financial structure of parishes). A question still remains about the distinctive contribution movements can make. When are movements more valuable than any other means of social change?

Movements are distinctive as a means of social change because they are actual environments which have formed around a new set of values or concerns. For instance, the institution of parish councils was accepted largely because of the diffusion of information (first stage) and then through institutional sponsorship (second stage). There was never much of a group of people (an environment) who developed common bonds because of their interest in parish councils. We would not tend to speak of "the parish council movement." Movements like the liturgical movement or the Cursillo or the CFM, however, have produced the changes they have in the Church by bringing a group of people together who have never been brought together before and forming a new environment.

Because movements form special environments, then, they can be most effective as forces for change when a special environment is needed for the change to occur. Parish councils were accepted because there was a preexisting environment (the environment of Church leaders) which was predisposed to accept them (by the Vatican Council). Parish councils were readily diffused without an environment, because they were the kind of thing which was acceptable to an environment which already existed. But the liturgical movement had to form an environment of its own to make any headway, because the environment of the Church as a whole at the time it began was not ready to accept what it advocated. Therefore, if there was going to be any fostering of an appreciation of the liturgy, it would have to be done in a special environment.

A movement, in other words, can effect a fundamental type of social change which would not have occurred without it. Because environments are effective in changing people's beliefs, attitudes, values, and behavior patterns, movements can be a force that can make more thoroughgoing reorientations than other means of social change. How effective they can be depends upon their strength as environments.

As we see the need for social change in the Church and face the many problems involved, it would make more sense many times to think of starting a movement than a program or an organization. For instance, the Church today is facing a problem among university students in their commitment to Christ. More headway has been made in this area through Cursillos, Cursillo-derived weekend programs, and the charismatic renewal than by most other efforts because they have had the appeal and impact of movements. Newman programs, university parishes, and student organizations have not been able to have the same effect. What is true in the area of university students is true in other areas where the Church faces a problem of overcoming environmental resistance.

If our concern is for the welfare of the Church, and if social change is needed in the Church, and if movements are one of the most effective sources of social change, then one of the most important pastoral tasks today is fostering movements in a way which produces constructive social change. Where movements which have a constructive purpose already exist, they should be encouraged and helped. But even more significantly, it is worth considering starting movements (or developing movements that already exist) to make headway in areas where the present environment in the Church or the world is resistant.

A common attitude toward movements (as toward communities) is that they just happen. Sometimes you can snuff them out at the beginning, but once they are under way, the only thing left is to just put up with them. Such an attitude has a grain of truth in it. Movements can rarely be gotten control of or directed the way an organization or a program can (although the Communists and other groups have developed techniques of getting control of social movements or of feeding off them and have often been successful). Once they begin, they are usually unstoppable. But movements can often be started to produce an improvement in the life of the Church. Moreover, once they have begun, they can often be channeled in ways that can be much more constructive to the life of the Church than if they had been left alone. In addition, often new movements can be started which can correct the deficiencies of the older ones.

The Cursillo movement is an interesting example of how movements can be begun to renew the Church. The Cursillo movement was deliberately begun in 1949 in Mallorca by a pastoral team of priests and laymen under the direction of a bishop. They set out to solve the problem of the alienation of the young from the

Church and the problem of the lack of Christian commitment in Christian organizations. They developed a method which has since given rise to a powerful international movement. In other words, the Cursillo movement was a movement which was started by Church leaders to make headway in an environment which was resistant to the Christian message and to overcome an imbalance in a previous movement in the Church (the Catholic Action movement).

Movements, then, can be made use of in pastoral work. They could become one of the most effective instruments in the work of the Church. They are more than just facts which have to be dealt with. They can be resources.

INTEGRATING MOVEMENTS

Movements, however, are not automatically resources. They can also cause problems. If movements are to become a constructive force in the life of the Church today, ways must be learned of avoiding or easing the problems which they cause. They must, in other words, be intelligently integrated into the life of the Church.

One reason movements cause problems is simply that they are forces for change. Any force for social change (institutional changes, programs, models) causes some of the same problems movements do. All agents of change trigger opposition and conflict, just because they are advocating something new and there will always be a variety of reasons why human beings resist change (from disagreement over values to simple inertia). Moreover, all efforts at change cause confusion and disorientation, because people need time and help to understand and adjust to something new. But there are special problems which seem to come with movements.

The fact that movements involve a special environment (groupings of people) with a specialized interest tends to cause the added problems of division, imbalance, and sectarianism. They cause division (not simply in the sense of differences of opinion but in the sense of group against group) because they uphold values which many in the community are unwilling to go along with, and because the presence of one group actively supporting something creates the tendency for an opposing group to form. They cause imbalance because they create environments which are specialized (centered around a certain value to the neglect of others). They cause sectarianism because sometimes the special groupings created isolate themselves from the rest of the Church and at times even leave the Church.

There is a great deal which can be done to avoid or obviate the problems caused by the presence of movements in the Church. First of all, many of the difficulties caused by the movements (and by any other means of social change) can be eased by the climate that surrounds them. If, for instance, the climate is one of lack of communication, whether the lack of communication is caused by the secretiveness of those involved in the movement or by the lack of openness of those who are not, there is room for a great deal of division, confusion and conflict to arise from rumor and ignorance. Lack of communication breeds prejudice. Fostering a climate of communication will overcome many of the problems movements give rise to.

Or, if the climate is one of rigidity, the tendency will be to form parties. Rigidity can exist on either side. Movements tend to become doctrinaire, parties of true believers, but those who are not in movements tend to form traditionalist parties, equally unbending. Where there is no absolute difference on value involved (which is usually the case with movements in the Church), attitudes of flexibility and experimentation can overcome tendencies to rigidity. If there is a feeling of openness to different approaches and a willingness to try an approach and see how it works, the disagreements can be put on an experimental basis (one open to factual verification, which disputes about absolute values are not).

Or, if the climate is one of suspicion rather than trust, there will be a tendency toward fear on both sides. Fear breeds fear, trust brings forth trust. When either the members of movements or others threaten the others' right to exist or call into question their motives, the natural response is fear. Many problems can be dealt with once there is enough trust for people to feel relaxed and secure in dealing with them.

Secondly, many of the difficulties caused by movements could be solved by the existence of adequately functioning basic Christian communities. One of the greatest sources of attraction movements today have is that they form communities. People who never felt a sense of involvement or personal relationship anywhere in the Church find it in movements. Consequently, they join movements because of the attractiveness of the communal life they find in the movement, not because they can see the value of what the movement is trying to foster.

Moreover, another result of the lack of adequately functioning basic Christian communities is the tendency of specialized communities to form in an imbalanced way. There are communities which exist solely for the sake of social action in which it would be scandalous to talk about prayer and vice versa. As the parish system becomes more and more inadequate, more and more specialized communities are being formed, and these communities are less and less in communication with other Christian groupings.

The formation of basic Christian communities which are open to change and to movements, but which would provide a basic community life, would do a great deal to stabilize the life of the Church today. The existence of adequate community life would mean that movements would not tend to produce groupings which are isolated or imbalanced. The very fact of the membership of the movements belonging to communities would counteract such tendencies. Basic Christian communities can be open to the influence of movements, and members of communities are in more of a position to consider movements on their merits and to avoid creating imbalanced special environments isolated from others.

Finally, many of the difficulties caused by movements could be solved by pastoral coordination. Since movements have institutions connected with them, often there will be conflicts and difficulties simply because the institutions overlap in purpose and there is no way of coordinating them for maximum positive effect. They end up being in competition with one another and with parish institutions in ways that are unnecessary.

About the years 1963 to 1965, as the Cursillo movement rapidly spread through the country, it had a structure which was worked out to be coordinated with the structure of Catholic Action in Spain. In the United States there was nothing like Catholic Action in Spain, but there was CFM which is a formation movement in many ways similar to the Cursillo movement and there were a variety of parish-based apostolic organizations (like the Legion of Mary and St. Vincent de Paul). Because of the similarity of structure, the Cursillo movement and CFM were in many places a drain on each other, since they competed for the time of the same lay leaders. There are a number of places in the country where the result of this was the weakening of lay involvement in the Church. Now something similar is beginning to happen with the charismatic renewal which is enough like both the Cursillo movement and the CFM to be another complicating factor in the situation. Some sort of coordination is needed and frequently never occurs.

The solution to the problem of climate and of coordination can be provided only by those who have positions of pastoral leadership in the Church. For instance, acceptance and understanding on the part of Church leadership is of great importance to those who belong to a movement. It can make all the difference in their loyalty to the Church and their willingness to work for it. The lack of it can lead to alienation among those who could be the strongest supports of the Church.

What follows are two typical scenarios based on actual situations which involved at least four movements in the Church (the CFM, the Cursillo movement, the charismatic renewal, and the peace movement). In situation A, a new movement enters a parish. At the beginning, the members feel that in being part of the movement they are helping the Church (because the Church needs this). They enthusiastically take part in the movement and just as enthusiastically (and naively) begin to spread it. They then receive a certain amount of opposition. They find themselves avoided by the pastor. They hear remarks he has made about them. Since most of them are not seasoned veterans of parish activities, they do not know the channels and protocol. They begin to feel alienated from the Church. They feel they have to make a choice between this new set of values with the community they have found through it and the institutions of the Church (the Church is now seen by them almost exclusively as an institution and not at all as a community). As some of their members opt for the pastor and the parish, the others harden more and more. If their community is strong enough, they go underground or leave the Church as a group. If their community is too weak to withstand the pressure, the individuals "hang loose" from the institutional Church or leave it altogether. The legacy is hard feelings on all sides.

In situation B also, a new movement enters a parish. The same sort of enthusiasm is generated both for the new movement and the Church. The same sort of reaction of fear, distrust, and opposition arises among other parishioners. The pastor, however, makes a point of finding out what is going on. He comes to the meetings of those who are part of the new movement in an attempt to understand the experience which is motivating these people. He reads the literature of the movement

170

in an effort to understand how this movement might fit into the life of the Church or the parish. Even before committing himself to a course of action, he begins to talk to the members of the movement about excesses and about situations of difficulty they are causing that they might not be aware of. He brings different groups together to talk about what is happening and what the reactions are. He directs the new group toward a place in the parish and, if he feels the group is making an important enough contribution, he encourages them openly. When the movement dissipates, if it does, there is at least no legacy of hostility toward the Church. If it does dissipate, many of the members of the movement become workers and leaders in parish activities.

Members of movements rarely have enough experience or vision to know how to integrate themselves into the life of the Church. The Church today is lucky that in a number of movements, which could be potentially the most disruptive, the leadership is in the hands of people who are committed to the overall good of the Church and not just to the set of values fostered by their movements. But it should be even more the role of the pastors within the Church to integrate movements into the Church than it is the role of the leaders of the movements. The pastoral office is the office which is concerned with the overall good of the whole Church (or parish or basic community). The leadership of the movements will most naturally be filled by the people who can most effectively advocate the cause which has given rise to the movement, and they will not be as sensitive or experienced in the problems of integration.

In order that there be men in the pastoral offices in

the Church who can provide the kind of direction which is needed, there has to be training for the pastoral office that will equip men both to foster the welfare of the whole Church and to be open to social change. They have to learn how to preside over the process of change in such a way that it builds up the Church and does not disintegrate it. They need to be pastors of their whole people, community formers.

There is also a need for consultant services for different movements. Neither the ordinary pastor in a parish nor the ordinary leader of a local group in any of the movements is capable without help of understanding the best way for movements to fit into the life of the local Church. Pastors would have to be experts on all movements, and the leaders would have to be experts on the whole parish. Consultant services are needed, first of all, within the movements for the leaders of the movements—services which can provide help for understanding the movement and its place in the Church. Consultant services are also needed locally (perhaps on a diocesan basis) so that the leaders of parishes and basic Christian communities can get the help they need to know how to make use of movements in the development of the parts of the Church for which they are responsible.

7

Setting Priorities

So far, this book has considered the basic approach to any pastoral planning in the Church today. It has recommended what could be called an environmental approach to forming the life of the Church. The application of this approach to the areas of parish renewal, spiritual renewal, leadership formation and social change has been sketched in. In other words, this book contains an overall strategy, a broad strategy, for the renewal of the life of the Church.

It might, however, be more precise to say that this book contains principles for a strategy for pastoral renewal in the Church. An overall approach has been sketched in a number of areas, but it is not yet a strategy, because it has not been stated developmentally. It is not clear from what has been said what the first step might be.

There is a need to know how to begin. One of the greatest problems facing workers in the Church today is knowing where and how to begin working. A great deal is known about the pastoral problems we face. Much theological and sociological and psychological data has been brought to bear on the situation. Too much, in fact. Knowing too much can lead to paralysis, because then the problems seem so large and there are so many possibilities of action that there is no logical place to start. When there is no developmental structure to what we know, the more we learn, the less effective we get.

There is a process to building something. This is true no matter what approach we take. Many efforts in the Church have failed because the processes of how to work were not understood. The traditional approach to religious education was very strong on teaching catechists the content of Christianity. Much effort was spent passing on content, only to learn that the catechists were ineffective because they did not know how to communicate the content they had. Not enough of a priority was put on method in the process of teaching.

It may be true that serving the poor in justice is, absolutely speaking, a greater priority for the Church than seminary training. It is, however, not necessarily the first thing to pay attention to. It is not necessarily a greater priority in the *process* of forming a Church which is adequate to everything that it is called to do. If the Church gives all of its energy to serving the poor in justice and does not direct any to training people who will be able to see this need and do something about it, the Church will make no progress. In other words, what is in itself more important is not necessarily the first thing we must turn our hand to. The most important things are not necessarily the first things *in pastoral priority*.

174

The process of pastoral renewal is a large topic. To talk about it adequately could take a book longer than this one. We have not attempted so much to explain "how to do it" as to sketch in the outlines of a new approach. It is, however, important to understand pastoral priorities and how they would function in an approach like the one we have developed. What follows are a few observations about priority and process which are implications of what has already been said.

1) TOP PRIORITY IS PERSONAL SPIRITUAL RENEWAL

Those who want to renew the Church have to begin with their own personal spiritual renewal. This is true whether the person concerned for renewal is the bishop or only a lay leader in some parish organization. Those who are going to work for the renewal of the Church have to seek a renewal of their knowledge of Christ and their life in him.

That the personal spiritual renewal of those who want to encourage pastoral renewal is the top priority follows from the analysis which has been given of the ways communities function. Communities come together for some purpose. The purpose, the source of unity and cohesiveness is the key to beginning the process of community formation. Therefore, concern for the purpose has to come first, because it is only through that which draws a community together that anything can happen. If a pastoral renewal is going to follow an environmental dynamic, that which begins the process (centering on that which is the reason for the existence of the community) has to be the first concern.

In other words, if we want a renewal of the Church,

the first step has to be turning more deeply to God. If those who want to work to renew the Church do not pray together and study the word of God together, if they do not tell others about Christ and put him in the forefront of their concern, they will not be effective. They may be able to do something which may make some contribution to humanity, but they will not strengthen the Church. Their efforts will not have behind them enough of a reason for Christianity to exist to motivate people to be concerned with the Church.

The moment at which a process of Christian renewal begins is the moment when one person or group of people can say, "It works! It's worthwhile!" When they have something themselves, and when they have the conviction that they have something, they can begin to work. Those who do not have a genuine conviction about Christianity lack the force or direction which makes them effective in Christian renewal.

Probably the second step in a process of Christian renewal comes when those who have dedicated themselves to working on it succeed in sharing what they have found for themselves with others. That is a sign that they have matured enough in what they themselves have to begin to be effective in leading others to find such a renewal. The second step may begin only moments after the first. Or it may take a while. But it is almost as important as the first.

2) THE SECOND PRIORITY IS TO FIND MEN OF GOD WHO CAN DO THE JOB

The second priority should be to find others who can work effectively at the process of pastoral renewal.

176

This is the second priority because it is men who build communities. Communities (and movements) form around their leaders, and they are usually as strong as their leaders. Without the right men the whole process cannot get off the ground.

In concrete terms, "finding men of God who can do the job" means building up a team of people who can work together on the problems of some part of the Church—people who can pray together, who can share their Christian lives together, who have a common vision of how to work to renew the Church. Little will be achieved without a unified group of workers. Any efforts which can be directed to increasing this group of workers is an effort which will multiply results.

3) THE THIRD PRIORITY IS TO BUILD BASIC CHRISTIAN COMMUNITIES

If the formation of basic Christian communities is going to be the approach of the future, those working on pastoral renewal have to begin forming such communities very early in the process. People will understand what a basic Christian community is only with difficulty if they cannot experience one. Workers will not easily understand how to build communities if they cannot have the experience of being part of one. It will be difficult for leaders in the process of Christian renewal to grasp what they are aiming at if they cannot see instances of what will be at the end of the process. People learn what needs to be done from the experience of seeing it happen. Once a person has experienced how a basic Christian community can work, he can think about what has to be done to get them to exist more and more.

In short, pilot projects and model centers are needed. Men have to be set to work to build basic Christian communities and once they are in existence, they will produce more workers who can do the same thing. Moreover, others can be sent there to be trained in how to do it. Once the parish of San Miguelito was formed in Panama, it became a means of opening up many people to new approaches to forming parish life. Many have seen there what they could only imagine before, and, in seeing it, they understood more about it (including the fact that it was actually possible).

The process has to begin by putting the emphasis on community formation, not on programs or activities. If what is needed is forming communities which make it possible for a person to live a Christian life, the beginning is to actually have such a community. A person cannot begin by forming structures and programs and expect communities to come out of the hopper on the other end. Communities grow, they are not produced. If a process of renewal does not begin with an environmental approach, it will probably never get to one.

In getting started, the impetus given by movements can be used. Movements generate environments and, with skill, these can be formed into basic Christian communities. Once a group of people has a new dedication to Christ and is willing to put a great deal into living as Christians, they are ready to be the nucleus of a basic Christian community. Movements can provide a ready impetus where otherwise the process of forming a community might take many years of scratching to start.

Setting Priorities

COORDINATED NEEDS

The above three priorities are requirements for beginning a pastoral renewal. There also are needs which have to be met at the same time a pastoral renewal is beginning. One such need is the need to maintain the present situation. The Church is, as a matter of fact, effective to a remarkable degree in keeping people alive, at least to a minimal level, as Christians. The present membership of the Church is a vast resource to work from—even if we cannot make full use of it at the moment. Maintenance of the present situation has to be part of the considerations, even though it would be fatal if that were all that were to be done (because the present structure of the Church is getting weaker, and something has to be done to make an improvement in the situation). Maintenance in the present and building for the future have to go on at the same time.

Another need that has to be met is the need to change the present institution. If there were in the Church today an effective approach to forming community life, with an effective way of forming Christian leaders, it would have difficulty gaining the support of the Church as a whole. The old structure still molds people's thinking to a great degree. It does so less and less each year but, nonetheless, the Church today is not ready to accept a whole new approach (even if the new approach were less radical than the one outlined above).

The present structure of the Church has to be made more flexible and open to changes, and it has to become more capable of profiting from them. If the change is not made in the present structure now, by the time a new approach evolves, the new approach will be of little profit to the Church as a whole. In other words, the fact that institutional change is not the main priority in meeting the pastoral needs of the Church does not mean that it is not important. Fortunately it is happening, and it is happening increasingly.

THE PROCESS

What we have been talking about is a process. The renewal of the Church has to be an organic growth. Environments and communities grow and develop, they are not (primarily) "worked out" and legislated. The formation of communities takes time, and the beginning is often the most difficult.

Because we are concerned with a process, there definitely are priorities we have to respect. Any change must begin with a group of people who have found a personal spiritual renewal. And every advance depends upon having men of God who can foster an environmental dynamic. And there do have to be pilot communities where the new forms are actually in operation as models for others. If the structures of the Church are changed without having pilot communities which embody a new approach, the institutional change will be no help (it will only help the Church to wither away more decorously). If the pilot communities are formed without the right kind of leadership, they will never get off the ground. If there is an attempt to recruit and form leadership without an initial core of men who have found Christianity to work for themselves and who can testify to the reality of Christ and the difference he makes, the leadership will have no vision and no effectiveness, nothing to pass on. There are unquestionably priorities.

Setting Priorities

There are priorities, but they are not the kind of priorities that are over and done with. In building a house it is possible to build the foundation first, and then stop building the foundation and put up the frame. Once the first step is accomplished, there is no need to come back to it. But an organic process is different. It may be true that the body has to be built strong before a man can work (building strength is temporally prior). But if a man dedicates 15 years to eating to build up his strength and then does not eat after that, his body will soon die. Maintaining strength has to be an ongoing part of the process. It is not possible, in Church renewal, therefore, to dedicate the first five years to personal spiritual renewal and then go on to finding leaders and give no more attention to personal spiritual renewal. Anyone who takes that approach will soon find the whole effort wasting away. Personal spiritual renewal, finding leaders, and forming basic Christian communities have to be an ongoing part of the process of Church renewal.

TRANSITION

There is much life in the Church today, many blossomings of Christian community. There are beginnings of a new form of Church life. At the same time, there is a widespread feeling of need for something new. People feel that if the Church is going to be able to go on, a revolutionary new approach to Christianity is needed.

The new form of Church life will have to be a gradual growth. A new way of living and relating has to come into being. It can be fostered and helped in various ways, but it cannot be simply decided upon. It has to grow.

What has been suggested in this book is a reorientation in the life of the Church—a reorientation that will allow something new to grow and will allow the Church to profit from what is coming into being. The book does not tell how to do it. Such a book can be written, but there is also a need for people to understand the reorientation of attitude and approach which will be required before a new form of Church life can come about. Christian community is a vision and a spirit as much as it is a method and practice. Christian community involves a new image and hope for the Church.

8

Appendix
The Medellin Documents

In 1969 the Latin American bishops met at Medellin in Colombia and adopted a number of statements about the future of the Church in Latin America. In the course of those statements, they accepted many of the principles discussed in this book as the future approach for the Church there. Since these are the first official statements of the hierarchy of the Catholic Church to advocate certain of the main principles behind the approach developed in this book, they are reproduced here:

A. BASIC CHRISTIAN COMMUNITIES

"10. The Christian ought to find the living of the communion to which he has been called in his 'basic community,' that is to say, in a community, local or environmental, which corresponds to the reality of a homogeneous group and whose size allows for personal fraternal contact among its members.[1] Consequently,

---

1 The meaning of "basic community" in the Medellin documents is slightly different from the meaning given to the term in chapter 3. "Basic community" means, first of all, something like what we have called "environment." It only secondarily means structured Christian community. The recommendation of this section of the documents is to find societal environments within parishes or cities and to make those the locus in which basic Christian communities are formed. For our purposes it is important only to note that the documents are recommending forming basic Christian communities within parishes as a more basic structure of Church life.

the Church's pastoral efforts must be oriented toward the transformation of these communities into a 'family of God,' beginning by making itself present among them as leaven by means of a nucleus, although it be small, which creates a community of faith, hope and charity. Thus the Christian basic community is the first and fundamental ecclesiastical nucleus, which on its own level must make itself responsible for the richness and expansion of the faith, as well as of the cult which is its expression. This community becomes then the initial cell of the ecclesiastical structures and the focus of evangelization, and it currently serves as the most important source of human advancement and development."

"13. The foregoing exposition leads us to make of the parish a pastoral whole, vivifying and unifying the basic communities. Thus the parish has to decentralize its pastoral action with respect to locations, functions and persons, precisely in order to 'reduce to unity all the human diversities which are found in it and to insert them into the universality of the Church.'"

—(From: 15. *Joint Pastoral Planning*)

B. POSITIONS OF LEADERSHIP IN CHRISTIAN
   COMMUNITIES

"12. The essential element for the existence of Christian basic communities are their leaders or directors. These can be priests, deacons, men or women religious, or laymen. It is desirable that they belong to the community which they animate."

—(From: 15. *Joint Pastoral Planning*)

"33a) An indispensable factor in the formation of

deacons[2] will be the reciprocal interaction between them and the community. That is to say, that the candidate attains to the fullness of his formation by acting within the community, while the latter contributes to this formation . . . .

"b) The first concern of those responsible for the formation of deacons is to prepare them to become capable of fostering new communities of Christians, and encouraging existing ones so that the mystery of the Church be brought to fruition in them to an ever greater degree."

—(From: 13. *The Formation of the Clergy*)

---

2 The recommendations made here for the training of deacons are the same as many of those in chapter 6 for the training of priests. The Medellin documents have not gone on to apply them to the training of priests as well, because the bishops have not yet felt free to change from the traditional seminary system for the formation of priests and also because Latin American bishops are using deacons more and more to perform pastoral functions in the absence of enough priests and in the expectation that sometime in the near future they will be able to ordain them to the priesthood.

Bibliography

The following books are helpful for understanding more fully the approach outlined in this book.

Bonnin, Eduardo, *et al., The How and the Why* (abridged), Ultreya, Phoenix, 1966. Available unabridged only in Spanish entitled *El Como y el Porque,* published by Euramerica S.A., Apartado 36.204, Madrid.
The How and the Why is an early (1955) statement of the history and theory behind the Cursillo movement. It shows an understanding of many of the points in this book and talks about a movement in the Church and how it can function in the life of the Church.

Bravo, Francisco, "Laymen . . . Is What It Takes!" *America,* April 8, 1967. A longer account of the San Miguelito project can be found in a book by the same author in Spanish, *The Parish of San Miguelito in Panama,* in the Sondeos series put out by CIDOC in Cuernavaca.
This article is a good short account of the parish of San Miguelito. At the time of the article, San Miguelito was one of the most progressive experiments in the formation of a new approach to parish life—the formation of basic Christian communities. Although there are many such experiments throughout the Church (mainly in Latin countries), this is one of the few descriptions of one in English. It is a description of how many of the principles in this book were put into effect in one situation.

CELAM, *The Church in the Present-Day Transformation of Latin America in the Light of the Council* (The Medellin Documents), The Latin American Bureau, USCC, Washington, D.C., 1970.

The Medellin Documents are statements of the Second General Conference of Latin American Bishops. These statements recommend most of the principles enunciated in this book. In respect to pastoral thinking, the Latin American Church has been far in advance of the Church in the United States.

Clark, Stephen B., *The Purpose of the Movement,* The National Secretariat of the Cursillos in Christianity, Box 304, Reno, Nevada, 1969.

A short description of the Cursillo movement and its place in the Church. These articles describe some of the unique thrusts of the Cursillo movement and also illustrate its place as a movement in the broader Church.

Currier, Richard, *Agony and Ecstasy in Building Christian Community,* Liguorian Pamphlets, 1969.

A description of Father Currier's communion program in the Diocese of Lansing and the principles behind it. The pamphlet shows an awareness of many of the principles in this book, but does not talk about many others. He tries to solve the problem mainly through small groups in the neighborhood. The focus is not on the basic Christian community.

Delespesse, Max, *The Church Community, Leaven and Life-Style,* The Catholic Centre of St. Paul University, Ottawa, 1969.

A book by a Belgian priest who is one of the leaders of a movement for the renewal of community life. He describes how community life functions and the principles behind it as it is lived in a number of communities in Europe and Africa. The approach he recommends is remarkably similar to the one in this book and is another testimony to the familiarity of these ideas outside the United States.

Kenney, Carlton, *The Church Which Is His Body,* Rev. Carlton Kenney, P.O. Box 5036, Waco, Texas.

A pamphlet by a Protestant minister of an independent

Church. It is a scriptural study of the life of a Christian community. It illustrates from the world of sectarian Protestantism the same principles.

Martin, Ralph, *Unless the Lord Build the House* . . . Ave Maria Press, Notre Dame, 1971.

An essay on the need for spiritual renewal in the Church today. It develops the functional importance of religious renewal and how that can be achieved.

Nee, Watchman, *The Normal Christian Church Life,* International Students Press, Washington, D.C., 1962.

A book by a Chinese involved in missionary work before World War II. Like the Kenney pamphlet, it illustrates many of the principles in this book, but from the thought patterns of evangelical Protestantism and from a missionary situation.

Ranaghan, Kevin and Dorothy (eds.), *As the Spirit Leads Us,* Paulist Press, Paramus, N.J., 1971.

A collection of articles by participants in the charismatic renewal. These articles illustrate the attempts to integrate a new movement into the life of the Church. Those which are most relevant to the area discussed in his book are: "Charismatic Renewal in the Church," "Life in Community," "Three Charismatic Communities," "Charismatic Leadership," and "Charismatic Renewal and the Church of Tomorrow."